BEYOND POLITE JAPANESE
A DICTIONARY OF JAPANESE SLANG AND COLLOQUIALISMS

BEYOND POLITE JAPANESE
A DICTIONARY OF JAPANESE SLANG AND COLLOQUIALISMS

Akihiko Yonekawa

translated by
Jeff Garrison

Kodansha International
Tokyo • New York • London

Distributed in the United States by Kodansha America, Inc., 114 Fifth Avenue, New York, N.Y. 10011, and in the United Kingdom and continental Europe by Kodansha Europe Ltd., 95 Aldwych, London WC2B 4JF. Published by Kodansha International Ltd., 17-14 Otowa 1-chome, Bunkyo-ku, Tokyo 112, and Kodansha America, Inc.

95 96 97 98 99 5 4 3

ISBN 4-7700-1539-9

CONTENTS

PREFACE

It is not necessarily true that textbookish Japanese is the same as the Japanese spoken daily throughout Japan. Or, to put it differently, the language of the people is necessarily not the language of the textbooks. There are, of course, many cogent reasons for this, as well as some reasons that are perhaps not so cogent. In any case, the present book proposes to help you, the student, go beyond the language of the textbooks by offering a number of useful, meaningful, and interesting words and phrases that are generally unavailable in the school curriculum—at least not with the meanings given here. In short, this book aims to help the student to acquire (in a relatively easy manner) vocabulary that would otherwise require years upon years of Japanese residency.

The entry words and phrases are all colloquial or slang. "Colloquial" means, of course, that they are more characteristic of the spoken language than the written. It also means, secondarily, that their meanings have occasionally taken on slightly different nuances from what is considered standard. Many of these words have already been adopted into large Japanese-language dictionaries; others have not. The criteria for inclusion in this book are several: frequency of use, usefulness, and sheer interest. The last aspect, "interest," I feel is important, for an interest in words is a strong stimulus to learning a language.

The slang included here is, for the most part, traditional slang. It has been accepted as slang for a long time, and will likely retain that status for decades to come. This is the slang that one hears in movies or reads in novels, and thus is most likely to be reinforced through those media as well as "on the street." It is also the slang that will be most understood if the reader chooses to put it into practice. Other slang included here is more contemporary, popular among high school and university students, but even then I have tried to select items that will be long-lived.

Longevity, in fact, has set the tone for the book in many crucial ways. It seemed to me that students who want to get closer to the vernacular might first wish to start with what is fairly established rather than with what is ephemeral, transient, and fugitive. Naturally, the fleeting can be fascinating, just as the historical can. But putting

7

first things first is not a bad rule in language learning, and so I decided to deal with more basic vocabulary in this area rather than being led astray by the less substantial.

The book has been divided into ten chapters: seven of which focus on meaning, three on form. The seven categories represented by the first seven chapters are largely arbitrary: many words could just have easily been placed in one or another of a number of chapters. Nonetheless, it still seemed better to group the words (no matter how unscientifically) according to content rather than simply listing them in alphabetical order. This arrangement, hopefully, will give the reader something to focus on in terms of content as well as provide an occasional opportunity to compare words of similar meaning.

The construction of each entry is fairly simple: 1) the entry word romanized, 2) the common (not sole) Japanese orthography, 3) the literal meaning, 4) English definitions or equivalents, 5) the sample sentence or sentences in Japanese, romanization, and English translation, 6) a comment or note when called for.

All of the above is pretty straightforward. Only the "literal meaning" perhaps needs additional explanation. Sometimes this meaning can be taken literally: e.g., where *nōtarin* is "short-of-brains." In other cases, the literal meaning tries to take a step back in the evolutionary history of the word to give a prior (dead or alive) meaning which clarifies the present one. Sometimes the step taken back is a short one, sometimes longer. In other cases, the literal meaning, for want of anything better, simply attempts to give a feeling for the Japanese word or phrase, either in terms of sound or meaning, and sometimes, more ideally, in both. In whichever case, however, "literal meanings" are to be seen as nothing more than as tools for coming to grips with the entry in question; they are not to be taken as viable translations or authenticated etymologies. This is not to say, of course, that they are fabrications without basis in fact (even given the uncertain state of Japanese etymology). A look at some of the better Japanese-language dictionaries will verify this point.

As far as the English translation is concerned, it strives for equivalency rather than literal meaning. In other words, in its attempt to convey the Japanese nuances, the English concentrates on the rendering of whole sentences rather than individual words. This is perhaps inevitable in translation of this sort, since the tone of colloquial Japanese is often determined by verb endings and sentence-ending particles—parts of speech that cannot be transferred as-is into English. Thus a particular Japanese sentence might be composed of unexceptional verbs and nouns etc., but still have a strong colloquial or slangy flavor due to the conjugations and particles. A literal translation of such sentences couldn't possibly capture the meaning of the originals, even though each word were painstakingly translated. In many cases the English provides not natural renditions of the Japanese, but rather an approximation of what English speakers might say in a similar situation; here again equivalency has taken precedence over literalness. Further, some of the English idioms appearing here might be termed "international" in that they are held in common throughout the English-speaking world. Many others, though, are strongly American, as is the tone of the book as a whole. It would be nice if colloquial or slangy Japanese could be translated into a variety of colloquial or slangy English that had currency with speakers of English throughout the world, but such an undertaking at this point in time seems highly dubious, if not downright impossible.

In general, I have assumed that the reader of this book has already mastered the fundamentals of the language. Thus not everything is explained. The reader I have in mind already knows that the standard word for "to eat" is *taberu,* and thus I have not bothered to mention this fact in the entry for the colloquial *kuu.* This approach was adopted, first of all, so as not to bore the reader unnecessarily but also as a space-saving device.

Finally, it is my hope that the present book will prove of use to the struggling student. All words require care in use, and the words and phrases in this book are no exception. There will be some that the student will instantly see can be put to immediate use. Others require precisely the right moment and situation, and will perhaps be more useful as part of your passive vocabulary rather than the active. All that, of course, is left to the reader's discretion.

This book could not have been written without a good deal of help, and I would particularly like to thank the translator, Jeff Garrison, and Taro Hirowatari, Michael Brase, Chikako Noma, and Shigeyoshi Suzuki at Kodansha International for all their efforts on the book's behalf.

People:
Nuns, Kettles, and Hungry Spirits

aitsu (あいつ) "that guy" N [Colloquial third person singular, used in expressions of affection, anger, and contempt] he, guy, dude, sucker.

あいつとは小学校時代からの友達さ。あいつはいいやつなんだ。

Aitsu to wa shōgakkō-jidai kara no tomodachi sa. Aitsu wa ii yatsu nan da.

Dude and I've been tight since grade school. He's a good guy.

おれが盗んだんじゃないよ。あいつだよ。あいつに決まっているよ。

Ore ga nusunda n' ja nai yo. Aitsu da yo. Aitsu ni kimatte iru yo.

No way I ripped that off, man. That sucker's the one that did it. You can bet on that.

ama (尼) "nun" N Broad, bitch, crack, cunt, dame, skirt, slut.

自分で失敗しておいて謝らないなんて、おまえも強情な尼だぜ。

Jibun de shippai shite oite ayamaranai nante, omae mo gōjō na ama da ze.

Refusing to say you're sorry after fuckin' up like that. You're one stubborn bitch, you know.

anchan (兄ちゃん) "little big-brother" N
1. [Familiar (usually second person) reference to one's older brother; now considered somewhat old-fashioned; approximate English equivalents include the diminutive form of the sibling's name].

あんちゃん、さっきからごはんだって、ママが呼んでるよ。

Anchan, sakki kara gohan datte, mama ga yonde 'ru yo.

Mom's been calling you. It's time to eat.

2. [Used by hoodlum types about or addressing any young man] ace, bud, buddy, Jake, Jack, pal, you.

そこのあんちゃん、ちょっとそこまで顔かしな。

Soko no anchan, chotto soko made kao kashi na.

Hey, Jack! Why don't we step outside for a minute.

☞ A contraction of *ani* (older brother) + *chan* (a contraction of *san*).

aneki (姉貴) "big sister" N [Familiar or respectful (usually second

person) reference to one's older sister. Approximate English equivalents include the diminutive form of the sibling's given name] sis.

いつも貧乏な僕には、姉貴だけが頼りなんだ。金貸してくれよ。

*Itsumo binbō na boku ni wa, aneki dake ga tayori nan da. Kane ka-
shite kure yo.*

You know I've been down on my luck a long time now and there's
no one else I can turn to except you, Sis. You've gotta loan me a
little bread.

☞ From the ordinary word for older sister, *ane*, plus the respectful *ki*.

aniki (兄貴) "big brother" N

1. [Familiar or respectful reference to one's older brother. Approximate English equivalents might include the diminutive form of the
sibling's given name] big brother.

パパが兄貴のマウンテンバイクに乗って行っちゃったよ。

Papa ga aniki no mauntenbaiku ni notte itchatta yo.

Dad took off on your mountain bike.

☞ Formed from the usual word for older brother, *ani*, plus the respectful *ki*.

2. Man, dude.

兄貴、お願いだから、おれを弟分にしてくださいよ。

Aniki, onegai da kara, ore o otōto-bun ni shite kudasai yo.

Come on, man. I'm begging you to take me under your wing and
teach me the ropes.

☞ Familiar reference among young men and yakuza to someone in the group who
is older or in a position of leadership.

anta (あんた) "you" N [Colloquial second person singular, used by
both men and women among their peers or when addressing someone of lower social position than themselves] you, ya.

私のことあんたって呼ばないで！私はあなたの母親なんだから。

*Watashi no koto anta tte yobanai de! Watashi wa anata no haha-oya
nan da kara.*

Don't be 'Hey, youing' me like that. I'm your mother.

☞ Corruption of *anata* (you). See also *kisama, omae, temē*.

atashi (あたし) "I" A [Colloquial first person pronoun used by
women and gays] I, me, yours truly.

ねえ、あんた。あたしだって女なのよ、たまにはやさしくしてよ。

Nee, anta. Atashi datte onna na no yo, tama ni wa yasashiku shite yo.

A woman likes to be treated nice once in a while, you know.

☞ Corruption of *watashi* (私).

atogama (後釜) "later kettle" N

1. Successor.

先週辞任した新井社長の後釜に、誰がなるか見ものだね。

Senshū jinin shita Arai-shachō no atogama ni, dare ga naru ka mimono da ne.

With Arai stepping down last week, it's going to be interesting to see who's next in line for the presidency (who gets the nod to take over for him).

2. One's second (third, fourth) wife.

亡くなった奥さんの後釜にきた人は、ずいぶん若い人なのね。

Nakunatta okusan no atogama ni kita hito wa, zuibun wakai hito na no ne.

The woman he married after his first wife died certainly is young, don't you think.

☞ Originally meant a kettle placed in the oven while heat remained from previous cooking.

babā (ばばあ) "old woman" Ⓝ

1. An old bag, biddy, haybag, hen, battle-ax, fossil.

ばばあ、じゃまだ！歩道で立ち話はやめてくれよ。

Babā, jama da! Hodō de tachibanashi wa yamete kure yo.

Move it, you old battle-ax! Quit standing around jawing in the middle of the sidewalk.

2. One's mother, old lady, old woman, the warden.

あのばばあ、いい年をしていつも厚化粧だから困るぜ。

Ano babā, ii toshi o shite itsumo atsu-geshō da kara komaru ze.

The old lady really embarrasses me with all the heavy makeup she puts on. She's no spring chicken.

bōzu (ぼうず／坊主) "monk" Ⓝ

1. [Irreverent reference to a Buddhist priest] sky pilot, Holy Joe.

お経もちゃんと読めない坊主がいるなんて信じられないわ。

Okyō mo chanto yomenai bōzu ga iru nante shinjirarenai wa.

Imagine a priest who can't even read a sutra right. Why I never...!

2. [Familiar or deferential reference to a young boy] little fella, little man, lad, squirt, kiddo, little bugger, little angel.

このファミコンはうちの坊主にぴったりのおもちゃだな。

Kono famikon wa uchi no bōzu ni pittari no omocha da na.

This Nintendo is just right for our little Johnny.

chinpira (チンピラ) Ⓝ

1. Twerp, smart aleck, pissant.

このチンピラめ！金も力もないくせして、口だけは一人前だな。

Kono chinpira-me! Kane mo chikara mo nai kuse shite, kuchi dake wa ichinin-mae da na.

You little smart-ass! No money to your name and you can't even fight your way out of a wet paper bag. But what a mouth!

2. Punk, petty hood; a juvenile delinquent, a juvey.

学生のくせにヤクザの手伝いなんかして、あんたチンピラなのね。

Gakusei no kuse ni yakuza no tetsudai nanka shite, anta chinpira na no ne.

You're nothing but a fuckin' punk, stooging for goons while you're still in school.

chongā (チョンガー) Ⓝ [Jocular or derogatory] bachelor, bach, stag, eligible man, available man.

妻もいなけりゃ子もいない、チョンガーで暮らすのが一番だね。

Tsuma mo inakerya ko mo inai, chongā de kurasu no ga ichiban da ne.

No kids and no ball and chain. I'll take the footloose and fancy-free life any day.

☞ In Korean, originally an adolescent hairstyle; later, used about men who retain this hairstyle after reaching adulthood.

dachi (ダチ) Ⓝ Friend, amigo, pal, buddy, homeboy, pardner, pard, sidekick, posse.

和雄のダチは、人情深いし面倒見がよくてほんとにいいやつだな。

Kazuo no dachi wa, ninjō-bukai shi mendō-mi ga yokute honto ni ii yatsu da na.

Kazuo's buddy's one stand-up dude, man. He'll see you through the shit, man.

☞ Abbreviation of *tomodachi* (友達); used almost exclusively by young people.

dafu-ya (ダフ屋) "tag man/woman" Ⓝ Scalper, digger.

マドンナのコンサートのチケットは、ダフ屋から買うしかないね。

Madonna no konsāto no chiketto wa, dafu-ya kara kau shika nai ne.

No way to get ahold of any tickets for the Madonna concert except through the scalpers.

☞ Reversal of *fuda*, which means "card" or "tag," to *dafu* and the addition of the suffix *ya*, which here indicates someone who is engaged in a certain business.

danna (旦那) "benefactor" Ⓝ

1. One's husband, hubby, the man of the house, the old man.

うちの旦那はのん気だから、いつまでも平社員のままなのよ。

Uchi no danna wa nonki da kara, itsu made mo hira-shain no mama na no yo.

My hubby's not exactly what you'd call a ball of fire, so he'll probably be on the bottom rungs of that ladder to success as long as he's with the company.

2. Mister, sir, Jack, bub, bud, buddy, chief, Joe, Mac, sport; [of and

to a policeman] officer.

サツの旦那、おれは無実ですぜ。もう勘弁してくださいよ。

Satsu no danna, ore wa mujitsu desu ze. Mō kanben shite kudasai yo.

Come on, officer, cut me a little slack, would ya. I'm clean. I swear it.

☞ From Sanskrit *dāna pati,* meaning "chief mourner; donor, or benefactor."

deka (デカ) "dick" Ⓝ Detective, flatfoot, gumshoe, sleuth, bloodhound, Sherlock.

あたしの兄貴はデカで、北海道の警察で凶悪犯の捜査をしているわ。

Atashi no aniki wa deka de, Hokkaidō no keisatsu de kyōaku-han no sōsa o shite iru wa.

My older brother's a detective on the force in Hokkaido, investigating violent (atrocious) crimes.

☞ In the early years of the Meiji Era plainclothesmen dressed in the contemporary equivalent of a trenchcoat, a style of overcoat known as a *kakusode* (square sleeves). Identified with their outfit, these sleuths were duly dubbed *kakusode.* Over time, and through the practice of creating slang words by a partial reversal of syllables, *kakusode* became *kusodeka,* and finally just *deka.*

furyō (不良) "not good" Ⓝ Juvenile delinquent, delinquent, juvie, juvey, punk.

髪を染めている生徒を、校長が不良だと決めつけちゃいけない。

Kami o somete iru seito o, kōchō ga furyō da to kimetsukecha ikenai.

School principals don't have any business branding students juvenile delinquents just because they go around dyeing their hair.

gaki (ガキ) "hungry spirit" Ⓝ

1. Kid, rug rat, crumbcrusher, anklebiter, a snotnosed kid, a teeny-bopper, a punk kid.

朝からガキがうるさくて、ゆっくり寝ることもできやしない。

Asa kara gaki ga urusakute, yukkuri neru koto mo deki ya shinai.

Guy can't get any shuteye with the brats making such a racket in the morning.

2. Asshole, dumbshit, lamebrain, no-neck.

このクソガキ、お前みたいなやつにオレの気持ちがわかるか。

Kono kuso-gaki, omae mitai na yatsu ni ore no kimochi ga wakaru ka.

What's a shithead like you gonna know about the way I feel?

☞ From the Buddhist word *gaki* (餓鬼) or "hungry spirit." The realm of the *gaki* is second from the bottom of the six fates awaiting all sentient beings who are not fortunate enough to escape the endless transmigration of souls by being enlightened.

gen'eki (現役) "active duty" Ⓝ

1. Still in school.

東大に現役で合格しちゃうなんて、山田君は頭がいいのね。

Tōdai ni gen'eki de gōkaku shichau nante, Yamada-kun wa atama ga ii no ne.

That Yamada must really have his act together to pass the entrance exam to Tokyo University while he is still in high school.

☞ Of aspiring young scholars who take exams for the next higher level of education (usually university) or those who actually pass such exams while still studying at a lower level. See also *rōnin*.

2. Active.

森監督は、現役のときは名捕手として有名だったんだってさ。

Mori-kantoku wa, gen'eki no toki wa mei-hoshu toshite yūmei datta n' datte sa.

Word has it that the manager of the team, Mr. Mori, used to be quite a famous catcher in his day.

gokutsubushi (穀潰し) **"grain-crusher"** N Loafer, bump-on-a-log, good-for-nothing, goof-off, fuck-off, goldbrick.

仕事もしないでブラブラしてるんじゃ、ただの穀潰しだぞ。

Shigoto mo shinai de burabura shite 'ru n' ja, tada no gokutsubushi da zo.

Out of work, just hanging out. You're nothing but a lazy good-for-nothing bum.

☞ Most commonly, but not exclusively, used about one's own son.

guru (グル) N Cohort, partner in crime.

兄弟ふたりでグルになって、親の私をだまそうっていうのね。

Kyōdai futari de guru ni natte, oya no watashi o damasō tte iu no ne.

So that's the way it is, huh? My own two children are in cahoots against me.

☞ One theory holds that *guru* derives from the English word "group," while another argues that it finds its origin in the onomatopoetic word *guru-guru*, which describes the activity of going around and around or forming a circle to discuss something, presumably for nefarious purposes. Formerly, criminal and delinquent use.

gyaru (ギャル) N (Single) gal, (little) babe, doll, fox, (little) lady, skirt.

河原町のディスコに行けば、ギャルは掃いて捨てるほどいるぜ。

Kawara-machi no disuko ni ikeba, gyaru wa haite suteru hodo iru ze.

Just drop by the discos in Kawara-machi. There are more little hard-bodies there than you can shake a stick at.

☞ From the English "gal." In use in Japan since 1979.

himo (ヒモ) **"a cord"** N Gigolo, honey man; pimp.

あいつはヒモだから、女に稼がせて自分は毎日遊んでるんだ。

Aitsu wa himo da kara, onna ni kasegasete jibun wa mainichi asonde 'ru n' da.

Guy's a gigolo. Nothing to do but send his woman off to work and hang out every day.

☞ From the primary meaning of *himo* (紐), cord, rope, or leash, comes the association with the organ grinder and his monkey on a leash and, hence, the way one of these characters makes his woman work the streets or elsewhere to support him.

hira (ヒラ／平) "flatness" Ⓝ Rank-and-file employee, the rank-and-file.

あの人は万年ヒラの安月給取りで、会社でも気楽なもんね。

Ano hito wa mannen-hira no yasu-gekkyū-tori de, kaisha de mo ki-raku na mon ne.

He's one of those hard-core rank-and-filers that'll be pulling in chickenfeed for the rest of his life, but he's living the life of Riley on the job.

iidashippe (言いだしっぺ) "fart broacher" Ⓝ Someone who starts something by mentioning it first.

この旅行、言いだしっぺはあんたよ。責任もって計画してよ。

Kono ryokō, iidashippe wa anta yo. Sekinin motte keikaku shite yo.

Hey, this trip was your bright idea! It's your responsibility to make the plans.

☞ From the idea that the farter is the first to know that a breach has been committed; thus, the first person to remark on the odor is likely the one who generated it. The last syllable, *pe*, is from the word for fart, *he*. *Iidashi* derives from the verb *iidasu*, "to speak out or broach." Written completely in kanji, the word is 言出庇.

inakappe (田舎っぺ) "country bumpkin" Ⓝ Hick, hayseed, bumpkin, yokel, rube, clodhopper, hillbilly, shitkicker.

今ごろカルダンの財布もらって喜ぶのは、田舎っぺだけだわ。

Ima-goro Karudan no saifu moratte yorokobu no wa, inakappe dake da wa.

No one gets worked up about having a Cardin wallet any more except a few hicks just off the bus.

☞ *Pe* is a corruption of the formerly common suffix to masculine names, *Hei* or *Bei* (兵衛). Similar in construction to "hillbilly"—"Billy from the hills."

iro-onna (色女) "colorful woman" Ⓝ Doll, fox, foxy lady, peach, babe, sexpot, turn-on, hot mama, hot tamale, hot stuff.

このバーのママは魅力的でなかなかの色女だね。

Kono bā no mama wa miryoku-teki de nakanaka no iro-onna da ne.

The chick that runs this joint is a hot little number.

☞ About women from twenty to around forty. In this case, *iro* (widely used in reference to love, sex, and physical relations between the sexes) can be translated as "sexy."

iro-otoko (色男) "colorful man" Ⓝ [Sexy man] hunk, he-man, stud, lady-killer; [joc.] God's gift to women, heartbreaker, Romeo.

よっ、色男！これまで何人の女を泣かせてきたんだい。

Yo', iro-otoko! Kore made nannin no onna o nakasete kita n' dai.

Hey, lover-boy, how many hearts have you broken?

☞ See previous entry for note on *iro*.

jijī (じじい) "old man" Ⓝ Old man, pops, old fossil, geezer, duffer, old coot, codger, buzzard.

なんだよ、じじい。文句があるならはっきり言えばいいだろう。

Nan da yo, jijī. Monku ga aru nara hakkiri ieba ii darō.

What's your problem, you old fart? If you've got something to say, spit it out.

jukunen (熟年) "ripe years" Ⓝ The prime of life.

パパは週末にクルーザーに乗って、熟年ライフを満喫してるわ。

Papa wa shūmatsu ni kurūzā ni notte, jukunen-raifu o mankitsu shite 'ru wa.

Daddy's really enjoying his middle age, going out on his cruiser on the weekends and stuff.

☞ Word created by the advertising firm Dentsu in 1979 to distinguish the mere middle-aged from those around fifty with status at their workplace, financial stability, and the time for leisurely activities.

kamisan (カミさん／上さん) "the one above" Ⓝ

1. The lady of the house, someone's wife.

あの八百屋のカミさんは、不景気で寝こんじまったらしいよ。

Ano yaoya no kamisan wa, fu-keiki de nekonjimatta rashii yo.

I hear that, what with business being bad and all, the greengrocer's wife isn't feeling well (has taken to her bed).

2. The missus, the better half, the ball and chain, the warden, the boss.

毎晩遅いってカミさんがうるさいから、今日は残業しないよ。

Maiban osoi tte kamisan ga urusai kara, kyō wa zangyō shinai yo.

My old lady's bitchin' about me coming home late every night so I'm not going to stick around and do any overtime tonight.

☞ Originally referred exclusively to a merchant's wife.

kamo (カモ) "duck" Ⓝ An easy mark, a sucker, dupe, pigeon, chump.

あいつ、マージャン弱いのに好きなんだから、いいカモだよね。

Aitsu, mājan yowai no ni suki nan da kara, ii kamo da yo ne.

He's no good at mah-jongg but he likes to play. Dude's the perfect patsy.

☞ From the proverb *kamo ga negi o shotte kuru*—the duck (鴨) that comes bearing the onions that will be cooked with it to make duck soup. See also *otokui-san*.

kanezuru (金づる) "money vine" Ⓝ Source of money, sponsor, meal ticket, pigeon.

研は直美を愛しちゃいない。金づるとして付き合ってるだけよ。

Ken wa Naomi o aishicha inai. Kanezuru toshite tsukiatte 'ru dake yo.

Ken doesn't give diddly about Naomi. It's her money he's after. / Ken's such a gold digger. He's just going out with Naomi to get his hands on her money.

kanojo (彼女) "she" Ⓝ

1. One's girlfriend, one's lover, one's main squeeze.

彼女といっしょになる決心したんだ。明日、結婚申し込むよ。

Kanojo to issho ni naru kesshin shita n' da. Ashita, kekkon mōshi-komu yo.

I've made up my mind to tie the knot. I'm gonna propose to her tomorrow.

2. Baby, mama, good-looking.

ねえ彼女、よかったらお茶しない?それかディスコでもいいよ。

Nē kanojo, yokattara ocha shinai? Sore ka disuko de mo ii yo.

Hey baby, how 'bout you 'n me having a cup of coffee together? Or we could check out a disco if that sounds better.

kare (彼) "he" Ⓝ

1. [A girl's] boyfriend, man.

こんどの日曜日はデートで、彼と軽井沢までドライブするのよ。

Kondo no Nichiyō-bi wa dēto de, kare to Karuizawa made doraibu suru no yo.

I'm going to Karuizawa with my boyfriend in his car this Sunday.

2. Guy, buddy, bub, friend, fellow, fella, compadre.

そこの彼、5分間だけこのアンケートに答えてくれないかなあ。

Soko no kare, gofun-kan dake kono ankēto ni kotaete kurenai ka nā.

Hey, man. Would you mind filling out this questionnaire for me? It'll only take five minutes of your time.

☞ Extension of meaning from the third person singular masculine pronoun.

kareshi (彼氏) "Mr. He" Ⓝ (A woman's) boyfriend, man.

あたし、スキー場に行ったときに、いまの彼氏と知り合ったの。

Atashi, sukī-jō ni itta toki ni, ima no kareshi to shiriatta no.

I met my current boyfriend at a ski resort.

☞ A well-intended, early-Showa coinage combining *kare* (he) with the respective *shi* (equivalent here to "Mr."), but which in popular usage soon assumed humorous connotations before evolving into the meaning given here.

kisama (貴様) "your honorable self" Ⓝ You [used affectionately among close male friends or as a term of abuse among men in general].

隠すなよ。貴様とおれとのあいだじゃないか。なんでも話せよ。

Kakusu na yo. Kisama to ore to no aida ja nai ka. Nan de mo hanase yo.

What are you keeping back? Come on, you and me are tight, aren't we? You can tell me.

小さな赤ちゃんを殴るなんて、貴様、それでも人間か？

Chiisa na akachan o naguru nante, kisama, sore de mo ningen ka?

What kind of a man are you, asshole, hitting a little baby like that.

☞ Originally a term of respect for one's superiors. See also *anta*, *omae*, *temē*.

kizumono (傷物) "damaged merchandise" Ⓝ An unmarried woman who has lost her virginity, damaged goods.

あんな男に引っかかって、うちの娘は傷物にされちまった。

Anna otoko ni hikkakatte, uchi no musume wa kizumono ni sare-chimatta.

It really pisses me off to think my daughter got her cherry popped by a guy like that.

koitsu (こいつ) "this guy" Ⓝ
1. He, my man, this mother.

こいつは遊ぶのが好きで、仕事をしたがらない困った人間だぜ。

Koitsu wa asobu no ga suki de, shigoto o shitagaranai komatta ningen da ze.

I don't know what to do about my man here. He has trouble buckling down 'cause he'd rather be out having a good time somewhere.

2. This, this thing, this stuff.

こいつはうまいコーヒーだ。どんな豆を使っているんだろうか。

Koitsu wa umai kōhī da. Donna mame o tsukatte iru n' darō ka.

This is some great coffee. Wonder what kind of beans they use.

kyaba-suke (キャバスケ／キャバ助) "Cabaret Mary" Ⓝ A woman who works in a cabaret; a college girl who wears heavy makeup and flashy clothes.

そんなキャバスケみたいに派手な化粧はやめたほうがいいよ。

Sonna kyaba-suke mitai ni hade na keshō wa yameta hō ga ii yo.

You'd be better off if you didn't put on so much makeup that you look like a cheap whore.

☞ Portmanteau word formed from the *kyaba* of *kyabare*, the word for cabaret, and *suke*, here a derogatory word for "woman" (though *suke* in other combinations can also refer to men).

kyaria-ūman (キャリアウーマン) "career woman" Ⓝ A woman who works for a living, a working girl.

仕事をバリバリこなすキャリアウーマンに、あたし憧れちゃう。

Shigoto o baribari konasu kyaria-ūman ni, atashi akogarechau.

That's the way I see myself someday, out on my own in the world, a working woman.

madogiwa-zoku (窓際族) "window-side tribe" Ⓝ An employee, usually middle-aged or older, who is on the payroll but has no specific duties and has been relegated to a desk by a window somewhere in the company; deadwood, useless employee.

会社で仕事もなくお茶飲んでるだけの窓際族にはなりたくない。

Kaisha de shigoto mo naku ocha nonde 'ru dake no madogiwa-zoku ni wa naritaku nai.

I'll tell you, I hope I don't end up sitting by a window somewhere in the company, drinking my tea at a clean desk.

☞ Since 1978.

ōbī (O B) Ⓝ Old boy, grad.

今度の試合はOBも見に来るから、気合いを入れていこうぜ。

Kondo no shiai wa ōbī mo mi ni kuru kara, kiai o irete ikō ze.

Some guys who used to be on the team are coming to see the next game, so whaddaya say we get out there and give it our best shot.

☞ Acronym formed from the "o" and "b" of the English "old boy."

oban (おばん) Ⓝ Bag, battle-ax, old hen, bat, old crow.

おばんのくせして、エステなんかに通うのやめなさいよね。

Oban no kuse shite, esute nanka ni kayou no yamenasai yo ne.

Hey, you're no spring chicken, you know. Don't you think you ought to lay off the upscale beauty salons?

若いのに腰が痛いなんて、あんたももうおばんだな。

Wakai no ni koshi ga itai nante, anta mo mō oban da na.

A backache at your age? Guy'd think you were over the hill or something.

☞ Corruption of standard word for a middle-aged woman, *obasan*. By removing the *sa* from the honorific suffix *-san*, disrespect is implied.

ochikobore (落ちこぼれ) "spillover" Ⓝ

1. A slow learner, a student who can't keep up with the class; a drop-out.

おれは小さいころから悪ガキで、クラスの落ちこぼれだったね。

Ore wa chiisai koro kara warugaki de, kurasu no ochikobore datta ne.

I used to fool around a lot in school when I was a kid so I was always at the bottom of the class.

2. A person who can't adapt, someone who gets left behind.

パパはエリート社員としては落ちこぼれだけど、あたしは好き。

Papa wa erīto-shain toshite wa ochikobore da kedo, atashi wa suki.

Dad may not measure up as one of the elite in his company, but I love him just the same.

☞ Common use in academia since 1971.

ōjī (O G) Ⓝ A (female) grad, a former (female) member of a club or other group.

クラブ創立20周年の記念にOGだけのパーティーをやりましょうよ。

Kurabu-sōritsu nijusshūnen no kinen ni ōjī dake no pātī o yarimashō yo.

What do you say to having a party to commemorate the twentieth anniversary of the founding of the club, only inviting women who used to be members?

☞ From the "o" and "g" of the Japanese English coinage "old girl," the female counterpart of "old boy."

ojamamushi (お邪魔虫) "pesky insect" Ⓝ Third wheel.

ここにいたらふたりのお邪魔虫になるから帰ろうかな。

Koko ni itara futari no ojamamushi ni naru kara kaerō ka na.

I guess I'd better be getting along. Don't want to cramp your style or anything.

ojin (おじん) Ⓝ Derogatory word for a middle-aged man or any other younger male who acts like one; guy, man, old man, scumbag.

最悪、聞いて。いやらしいおじんに通勤電車のなかで触られたわ。

Saiaku, kiite. Iyarashii ojin ni tsūkin-densha no naka de sawarareta wa.

Like, listen to what happened to me. It was so gross. Some grody old man copped a feel on my way to work on the train.

高校生なのに演歌ばかり聴くから、おじんだって言われるんだ。

Kōkō-sei na no ni enka bakari kiku kara, ojin datte iwareru n' da.

Just 'cause I'm still in high school and like to listen to enka, they call me an old fogy.

☞ Corruption of *ojisan*, the standard word for a middle-aged man. Removal of the *sa* from the honorific suffix *-san* serves to imply disrespect.

okama (オカマ) **"honorable kettle"** N [Used either about a homosexual or a feminine man] queer, fag, faggot, fairy.

オカマじゃあるまいし、グラス持つのに小指立てんじゃねえよ。

Okama ja aru mai shi, gurasu motsu no ni koyubi taten ja nē yo.

What are you, a faggot, man? What are you doin' holding your glass with your little finger sticking out like that?

☞ From the belief that the human posterior resembles a kettle comes the slang usage of *okama* (御釜) to mean "rear end" and hence one who prefers anal intercourse with a person of the same sex.

okuri-ōkami (送り狼) **"a see-you-home wolf"** N A man who feigns thoughtfulness by offering to see a girl home, only to try to molest her once he gets in the door.

やさしそうな顔をして、やっぱり幹男も送り狼だったわけね。

Yasashisō na kao o shite, yappari Mikio mo okuri-ōkami datta wake ne.

Mikio is so sweet-looking, but in the end it was the same old date rape deal with him, too.

ōkura-shō (大蔵省) **"Ministry of Finance"** N [Usually in reference to one's wife] the paymaster, the boss.

うちの大蔵省は厳しくて、一日に500円しか小遣いくれないんだ。

Uchi no ōkura-shō wa kibishikute, ichinichi ni gohyaku-en shika kozukai kurenai n' da.

My old lady's pretty tight when it comes to doling out the money. Five hundred yen a day is all the spending money she allows me.

☞ From the notion that a wife who controls the purse strings in a family is like the central government's Ministry of Finance in that she determines where the money goes.

ōeru (O L) N A working woman, a working girl, a businesswoman.

私は大学を卒業したら、2、3年ぐらいOLをするつもりなの。

Watashi wa daigaku o sotsugyō shitara, ni-san–nen gurai ōeru o suru tsumori na no.

I plan to work for two or three years after I graduate from college.

指示されたことをするだけがOLの仕事だと思ったら間違いよ。

Shiji sareta koto o suru dake ga ōeru no shigoto da to omottara machigai yo.

You're wrong if you think all a working woman has to do is what she's told.

☞ From the Japanese English coinage "office lady." Since 1963.

omae (おまえ／お前) **"honorable front"** N [Used by men to peers or those younger than themselves. Considered abusive when used by men to their superiors and vulgar when used by women] you.

おれとおまえの仲じゃないか、そんな水くさいこと言うなって。

Ore to omae no naka ja nai ka, sonna mizu-kusai koto iu na tte.

Come off it, man. You can let your hair down in front of me.

お父さんはお前のためを思って言っているんだぞ。わかっているか。

Otōsan wa omae no tame o omotte itte iru n' da zo. Wakatte iru ka.

Dad's just saying that for your own good, you know. Can't you get that through your thick skull?

☞ Originally a term of respect for one's superiors. See also *anta*, *kisama*, *temē*.

omawari (お巡り) "honorable going-around" N A cop, a pig [when the honorific suffix *-san* is added the word becomes somewhat respectful as well as familiar].

お巡りに見つかるとやばいぜ。そろそろずらかろうや。

Omawari ni mitsukaru to yabai ze. Sorosoro zurakarō ya.

The shit'll hit the fan if the cops find us here. Let's split.

☞ Combination of the honorific prefix *o* and *mawari*, which means "going around" or, by extension, making the rounds or walking one's beat. See also *satsu*.

ore (おれ／俺) "I" N [Used by men among friends or in the presence of subordinates; rougher than *boku*] I, me, number one, numero uno, the kid.

ほら、俺の言った通りだろ。俺の言うことはいつも正しい。

Hora, ore no itta tōri daro. Ore no iu koto wa itsumo tadashii.

See, what did I tell you. Is the dude always right, or what.

☞ Used by both men and women until the mid eighteenth century.

ōrudo-misu (オールドミス) "old miss" N An old maid, a spinster.

結婚のことを真剣に考えないと、オールドミスになっちゃうわ。

Kekkon no koto o shinken ni kangaenai to, ōrudo-misu ni natchau wa.

If you don't give some serious thought to getting married, you'll end up an old maid.

☞ Japanese English coinage "old miss." See also *urenokori*.

ossan (おっさん) N [Used to address middle-aged and older men] mister, buddy, bud, Jack.

おっさん！楊枝をくわえたまま歩き回るの、頼むからやめてくれ。

Ossan! Yōji o kuwaeta mama arukimawaru no, tanomu kara yamete kure.

Hey, Mack! How about not walking around with a toothpick stuck in your mouth like that, huh. Whaddya say?

☞ Corruption of *ojisan*, a standard reference to any avuncular type.

otokui-san (お得意さん) "honorable prosperity" Ⓝ

1. A regular customer.

あちらはうちのお得意さんで、いつもたくさん買ってくれるよ。

Achira wa uchi no otokui-san de, itsumo takusan katte kureru yo.

That guy over there is one of our best customers. He invariably buys a great deal.

☞ Synonymous with *tokui-saki* (得意先).

2. A pushover, an easy mark.

また、将棋で負けたの？あんたは山田さんのお得意さんだね。

Mata, shōgi de maketa no? Anta wa Yamada-san no otokui-san da ne.

Got whipped at shogi again, huh? Yamada must just love playing you.

pūtarō (プータロー／風太郎) "Taro of the Wind" Ⓝ A loafer, a goldbrick, a fuck-off, a drugstore cowboy.

太郎は学校でてから就職もしないで、プータローなんだってよ。

Tarō wa gakkō dete kara shūshoku mo shinai de, pūtarō nan datte yo.

Hear tell that old Taro's just been hangin' out since he got out of school.

☞ Longshoreman's argot. *Pū* from the Japanese for wind, *kaze*, or *fū*, in combination and the common masculine given name "Taro." Hence, a person who, like the wind, changes often and does not stay long in one place.

rōnin (浪人) "a wandering person" Ⓝ Someone who has failed entrance examinations and is presently out of school studying to retake them, someone looking for work, a ronin.

大学受験に失敗したら、1年浪人して、予備校に通えばいいさ。

Daigaku-juken ni shippai shitara, ichinen rōnin shite, yobi-kō ni ka-yoeba ii sa.

No sweat if I flunk the college entrance exams. I'll just cool my heels at a prep school for a year, that's all.

☞ Originally used during the Edo period about a masterless samurai.

sakura (サクラ) "cherry (blossom)" Ⓝ Shill, booster, plant, decoy, claqueur.

他の客がサクラとは知らず、つられて品物を買ってしまったよ。

Hoka no kyaku ga sakura to wa shirazu, tsurarete shinamono o katte shimatta yo.

I didn't know the other customers were shills and got duped into buying something.

☞ Street vendor's argot. From the notion that they come and go as quickly as the cherry blossoms do.

satsu (サツ／察) N The police, the man, the pigs.

あの男がサツだと知っていたら、仲間に誘ったりしねえぞ。

Ano otoko ga satsu da to shitte itara, nakama ni sasottari shinē zo.

No way I'd let that dude in on things if I'd known he was the heat, man.

☞ Yakuza and criminal argot. Shortened form of *keisatsu*, the standard word for the police. See also *omawari*.

senkō (先公) N [Derogatory word for a teacher] teach.

タバコ吸ってるところを先公に見つかって、停学処分くらった。

Tabako sutte 'ru tokoro o senkō ni mitsukatte, teigaku-shobun ku-ratta.

Some teacher caught me smoking and I ended up getting suspended.

☞ Coinage from the *sen* of *sensei*, the word for teacher, and the here derogatory suffix *kō*. Originally delinquent usage.

shayō-zoku (社用族) "the company tribe" N Employees living high off the hog on company money.

銀座で飲んでるような連中は、みんな社用族に決まってるわ。

Ginza de nonde 'ru yō na renchū wa, minna shayō-zoku ni kimatte 'ru wa.

No way all those people who go drinking in Ginza all the time are paying for it out of their own pockets. It's company money for sure.

☞ Play on a homonym meaning "sundowners" (斜陽族), the decadent upper class which was no longer able to keep pace with changes in society. Since 1951.

shin-jinrui (新人類) "new human species" N [A Japanese born after 1960, brought up on TV, and considered to be frivolous, unwilling to do more than the minimum to get the job done, and lacking organizational commitment] the new breed.

ちょっと怒られただけで会社辞めちゃうような新人類が大勢いるらしい。

Chotto okorareta dake de kaisha yamechau yō na shin-jinrui ga ōzei iru rashii.

Seems like there are a lot of younger workers who just up and quit their job if they get called on the carpet for anything at all.

☞ Since 1986. Antonym, *kyū-jinrui* (旧人類).

sukeban (スケ番／助番) "group (girl) boss" N The leader of a group of juvenile delinquent girls.

桜さんって今は普通のOLだけど、高校ではスケ番だったの。

Sakura-san tte ima wa futsū no ōeru da kedo, kōkō de wa sukeban datta no.

Sakura may be a regular working woman now, but she was a real hell-raiser when she was in high school.

☞ *Suke* is here a derogatory word for woman or girl and *ban* is the shortened form of *banchō*, the leader of a group of juvenile delinquents. Originally used among juvenile delinquents, in the common idiom since circa 1972.

temē (てめえ) "before the hand" Ⓝ

1. I, me, yours truly, number one.

てめえなんかも、年とってつまらない人間になっちまいました。

Temē nanka mo, toshitotte tsumaranai ningen ni natchimaimashita.

I've turned into a boring old fart in my old age.

2. You, fucker, dipshit, asshole.

てめえはこの話に関係ないんだから、引っ込んでろよ。

Temē wa kono hanashi ni kankei nai n' da kara, hikkonde 'ro yo.

This is none of your fuckin' business, asshole, so why don't you just butt out.

☞ Corruption of *temae* (手前). See also *anata*, *kisama*, *omae*.

tōshirō (とうしろう／藤四郎) Ⓝ An amateur.

あの新人はとうしろうのくせに、玄人顔負けの演技をするな。

Ano shinjin wa tōshirō no kuse ni, kurōto-kaomake no engi o suru na.

That new guy may be a rank amateur, but his acting sure puts the pros to shame.

☞ Partial inversion of the pronunciation of *shirōto* (素人), or amateur, with homophonic but arbitary kanji to simulate a given masculine name. Used among street vendors and the entertainment industry.

unchan (運ちゃん) "little driver" Ⓝ [Slightly offensive appellation for the driver of any large vehicle or vehicle for hire] a truck driver, trucker; a taxi driver, a hack, a bus driver, a bus jockey.

財布を忘れてタクシーに乗ったもんで、運ちゃんにどなられた。

Saifu o wasurete takushī ni notta mon de, unchan ni donarareta.

Cabbie laid into me when he found out I didn't have my wallet on me.

☞ *Un* is from *unten-shi* (運転士), the standard word for driver, plus the diminutive suffix *-chan*.

urenokori (売れ残り) "unsold goods" Ⓝ A single woman beyond the marrying age, an old maid, a spinster.

3人姉妹で長女のあたしだけが、まだ売れ残りなのよ。

Sannin-shimai de chōjo no atashi dake ga, mada urenokori na no yo.

The oldest of three sisters and I'm the only one who can't seem to get hitched.

☞ See also *ōrudo-misu*.

waru (ワル／悪) **"bad"** N Bastard, son of a bitch, bad dude, prick, bad ass.

飲み屋のツケを踏み倒すとは、君も相当なワルだな。

Nomiya no tsuke o fumitaosu to wa, kimi mo sōtō na waru da na.

You're quite a scumbag, aren't you, skipping out on a bar tab like that.

yabu (やぶ) **"thicket"** N A quack.

あそこの医者はやぶで病気が治らないって言うもっぱらの噂よ。

Asoko no isha wa yabu de byōki ga naoranai tte iu moppara no uwasa yo.

Word is that quack couldn't cure you if his life depended on it.

☞ Shortened form of *yabu-isha* (薮医者; "doctor in the thicket"), the kanji for *yabu* being based on folk etymology.

yarō (野郎) **"field man"** N Man, guy, dude, fucker, mother, bastard.

あの野郎、おれをなめやがって。そう簡単にだまされないぞ。

Ano yarō, ore o nameyagatte. Sō kantan ni damasarenai zo.

Fucker's trying to pull the wool over my eyes. Guess I'll have to show him that's easier said than done.

yāsan (やーさん) N Gangster, yakuza, hood.

どうしてヤーさんはパンチパーマとサングラスが好きなのかな。

Dōshite yāsan wa panchipāma to sangurasu ga suki na no ka na.

Whaddya suppose it is about sunglasses and tight permanents that the hoods dig so much?

☞ From the *ya* of *yakuza* and the honorific suffix *-san*.

yatsu (やつ) **"the guy"** N

1. [About people] man, guy, dude, gal, bitch; [about animals] sucker, son of a bitch.

おまえも変なやつだな。おれの指示どおり何故やらないんだ？

Omae mo hen na yatsu da na. Ore no shiji-dōri naze yaranai n' da?

What's gotten into you, anyway? Why don't you just do like I tell you to?

2. [About inanimate objects] it, one.

この雑誌、先週買ったやつと同じよ。あんた、ダブって買ったの？

Kono zasshi, senshū katta yatsu to onaji yo. Anta, dabutte katta no?

This is the same magazine you picked up last week. What did you go and do, buy two of the same thing?

3. A what-do-you-call-it, a what's-it, that thing called a …

おれ、太り過ぎだから、食餌療法というやつをやることになった。

Ore, futorisugi da kara, shokuji-ryōhō to iu yatsu o yaru koto ni natta.

They put me on one of those diet things because I've got to lose some weight.

4. He, she.

新しい営業局長は山田君か。やつにそんな大役が務まるのかね。

Atarashii eigyō–kyoku-chō wa Yamada-kun ka. Yatsu ni sonna tai-yaku ga tsutomaru no ka ne.

So Yamada's the new sales manager, huh? You think he's up to it?

Personality Types and Temperaments:
Bright Roots and Dark Roots

abazure (あばずれ) "place rubbing" Ⓝ A (real) bitch, a witch, a cunt, a bitch kitty.

おれの他にも男がいたなんて、あんなあばずれとはおさらばだ。

Ore no hoka ni mo otoko ga ita nante, anna abazure to wa osaraba da.

To think that there was another guy! I've had it with that two-timing bitch.

☞ *Sure* or *-zure* (from the verb *sureru*) means to rub against (often in the wrong direction). *Aba*, according to one theory, is a corruption of *oba* (お場; place), hence action that is inappropriate to the time and place. Formerly used of both sexes; now limited to women.

abunai (あぶない) "dangerous" Ⓐ [Of a situation or event] strange, weird, crazy; [of a person] off one's rocker, cracked, weird, a brick short of a load.

明け方までコンピューターゲームしているようなやつはアブナイ。

Akegata made konpyūtā-gēmu shite iru yō na yatsu wa abunai.

You've got to wonder about guys who stay up all night playing computer games.

aho (阿呆) Ⓐ Ⓝ Stupid, foolish, dumb, goofy; [the person] an airhead, a dummy, a dipshit.

ばか、あほ！おまえなんか嫌いだ。早く死んじゃえばいいんだ。

Baka, aho! Omae nanka kirai da. Hayaku shinjaeba ii n' da.

You stupid idiot! Where do you get off doing that shit? Just drop dead, huh.

うちアホやし、"まけといてえ" なんかよう言わんわ。(Kansai dialect)

Uchi aho ya shi, "maketoitē" nanka yō iwan wa.

I'm so stupid. It's all I can do to ask for a discount.

☞ In the Kansai dialect, *aho* suggests familiarity and affection rather than disdain. When coupled with the intensifying prefix *do* as in *do-aho*, however, it takes on an even stronger sense of disapprobation than does *baka* in the Tokyo dialect. *Aho* can also be written 阿房, but in either case the etymology is unclear. Also pronounced *ahō*. See also *baka*, *nōtarin*, *pā*, and *teinō*.

akeppiroge (明けっ広げ) "wide open" Ⓐ Open, frank, up front.

30

あいつ、あけっぴろげだから借金いくらあるかみんなが知ってる。
Aitsu, akeppiroge da kara shakkin ikura aru ka minna shitte 'ru.

The guy's such an open book that everyone knows how far in debt he is.

amaenbō (甘えん坊) "sweet body" N A pampered person, a spoiled child (brat).

あたしって甘えん坊だから、ひとりっきりじゃ変になっちゃう。
Atashi tte amaenbō da kara, hitorikkiri ja hen ni natchau.

If I didn't have someone to lean on, I think I'd go crazy.
☞ *Bō* is a personifying suffix.

amatchoroi (甘っちょろい) "sweet and simple" A Simplistic, corny, childish, half-assed.

そんな甘っちょろい考えで、本当に自活できると思ってるのかい？
Sonna amatchoroi kangae de, hontō ni jikatsu dekiru to omotte 'ru no kai?

You're just kidding yourself if you really think you can make it on your own with such a half-baked view of life.
☞ Corruption of *amachoroi*, a portmanteau word formed from *ama* of *amai*, meaning "sweet" or half-baked, and *choroi*, a word meaning "lax" or simple.

aruchū (アル中) N Alcoholism; an alcoholic, drunk, lush, juice head, juicer.

昼間っからお酒飲んで酔っぱらって、あの人はまるでアル中ね。
Hiruma kkara osake nonde yopparatte, ano hito wa maru de aruchū ne.

Anybody who starts tippin' 'em back during the day and gets drunk like he does has got to be an alky.
☞ Abbreviation of *arukōru-chūdoku* (alcohol poisoning). *Arukōru-izonshō* (アルコール依存症; alcohol dependency) is a less judgmental term for alcoholism enjoying increasing usage.

asobinin (遊び人) "play person" N An idler, a loafer, a lounge lizard.

彼は遊び人だから、六本木のディスコに行けば必ず会えるわよ。
Kare wa asobinin da kara, Roppongi no disuko ni ikeba kanarazu aeru wa yo.

All he ever does is hang out, so you can always catch him at a disco in Roppongi.

baka (馬鹿) "horse-deer" N A Stupid, dumb, silly; [the person] a fool, a knucklehead, a dope, a no-neck.

惚れた女にだまされて金まで盗まれるなんて、おれもバカだよ。
Horeta onna ni damasarete kane made nusumareru nante, ore

mo baka da yo.

I must have a hole in my head to get taken in and fleeced by a gal I thought I was in love with.

バカ、しつこいわ！あんたとは付き合わないって言ったでしょ。

Baka, shitsukoi wa! Anta to wa tsukiawanai tte itta desho.

Lay off (Come on), birdbrain! I already told ya there's no way I'm going out with you.

☞ *Baka* lacks strong derisive meaning in the Tokyo area, but is perceived to be much stronger in the Kansai area. The word is apparently derived from the Sanskrit. The kanji ("horse-deer") are only phonetic equivalents. See also *aho*, *nōtarin*, *pā*, and *teinō*.

boke (ボケ) "addled" N A numbskull, birdbrain, simp, turkey.

ボケ！おれの仕事場に電話するなって何度言ったらわかるんだ。

Boke! Ore no shigoto-ba ni denwa suru na tte nando ittara wakaru n' da.

You lamebrain, how many times I gotta tell you not to call me at work?

☞ From *bokeru* (惚ける; to be become bewildered, confused, out of touch).

boke-rōjin (ボケ老人) "addled oldster" N A doter, a senile old person.

隣のおじいさん、アルツハイマーなの。ボケ老人ね、かわいそうに。

Tonari no ojī-san, arutsuhaimā na no. Boke-rōjin ne, kawaisō ni.

It's so sad the way the poor old guy next door's losing his grip 'cause he's got Alzheimer's.

☞ See also note to previous entry. In general usage since 1980.

busu (ブス) N

1. A pig, dog, two-bagger.

あいつ、ブスだけど、すごく気立てのいいやさしい娘なんだ。

Aitsu, busu da kedo, sugoku kidate no ii yasashii ko nan da.

Gal may be uglier 'n sin, but she's got a great personality.

2. [Suffixed to a noun] bad.

あの女、顔もスタイルも悪くないのに、性格ブスなやつだ。

Ano onna, kao mo sutairu mo waruku nai no ni, seikaku-busu na yatsu da.

Can't complain about the way she looks or dresses, but let me tell you, she's one bitch.

☞ Pejorative. Etymological theories abound. One holds that *busu* is an abbreviation of *busuke* or "not good-looking" (ぶすけ[不美人]), and first used by juvenile delinquents. Another suggests that it derives from a homonymic kyōgen drama which takes its name from a deadly poison, *busu* (「ぶす(附子)」), hence, a face resembling that of a person who has just imbibed *busu*.

chakkari-ya (ちゃっかり屋) "cagey one" N Someone looking out for number one, especially financially.

彼女はちゃっかり屋で、誕生日の贈り物はお金にしてくれだと。

Kanojo wa chakkari-ya de, tanjō-bi no okurimono wa okane ni shite kure da to.

You know there are no flies on her when it comes to money, the way she asked for cash for her birthday.

☞ A combination of the adverb *chakkari* (shrewd) and *ya* (a suffix indicating a person marked by certain characteristics).

charan-poran (ちゃらんぽらん) "flimflam" A Irresponsible, loose, lax, ho-hum.

ぼくの上司はちゃらんぽらんで、いい加減な指示ばかりするよ。

Boku no jōshi wa charan-poran de, ii kagen na shiji bakari suru yo.

You can tell that my boss has an I-couldn't-give-a-shit attitude by the way he supervises us.

☞ Possibly a reduplication of *chara* (flam, fib, fibber) with *n* added for emphasis.

donkan (鈍感) "dull sense" A Dull, slow, out of it, thick. N A dolt, dope.

君はなんて鈍感なんだろ。彼女に男がいたって知らなかったの？

Kimi wa nante donkan nan daro. Kanojo ni otoko ga ita tte shirana-katta no?

You mean to tell me that you didn't even know there was another man? Where the hell have you been?

☞ See also *toroi*.

dora-musuko (どら息子) "fast-living son" N A lazy good-for-nothing son, profligate son.

うちのドラ息子は、遊んでばかりで、昨日も帰ってこなかった。

Uchi no dora-musuko wa, asonde bakari de, kinō mo kaette kona-katta.

That bum I call my son was out gallivanting around again last night and still hasn't come home.

etchi (エッチ) A Dirty, lewd, off-color. N A dirty (old) man, lech.

きゃあエッチ、なんであんたに触られなきゃなんないのよ！

Kyā etchi, nande anta ni sawararenakya nannai no yo!

Hey, what do you think you're doing? Get your hands off me!

☞ Used by young women. From the "h" of *hentai* (変態) or pervert. See also *sukebē*.

gametsui (がめつい) "chintzy" A Greedy, grasping, avaricious, money-grubbing.

借りた金に10割利子つけて返せだと、あんたもがめついね。

Karita kane ni jū-wari rishi tsukete kaese da to, anta mo gametsui ne.

You're one greedy mother, wanting your money back at 100% interest.

☞ A coinage in widespread usage since 1959.

gariben (ガリ勉／我利勉) "self-profit studies" Ⓝ A grind, nerd, geek, dweeb, pencil neck, smack. Ⓥ (*suru*) Crack (hit, cook) the books, kick ass, book it.

東大はガリ勉ばかりがいると思ったら、大間違い。昔の話だよ。

Tōdai wa gariben bakari ga iru to omottara, ōmachigai. Mukashi no hanashi da yo.

You're wrong if you think that there are just a bunch of nerds at Tokyo University. Those days are long gone.

hentai (変態) "transformed" Ⓝ Perversion; a pervert.

殴られて気持ちがいいなんて、ヘンタイの証拠だと思わないか？

Nagurarete kimochi ga ii nante, hentai no shōko da to omowanai ka?

Getting off on being beaten up proves that you're a pervert, wouldn't you say?

hesomagari (へそまがり) "bent belly button" Ⓐ Perverse, cantankerous, ornery, twisted. Ⓝ A crank.

ぼくのオヤジはへそまがりでね、褒められると機嫌が悪くなるんだよ。

Boku no oyaji wa hesomagari de ne, homerareru to kigen ga waruku naru n' da yo.

My dad's a little quirky the way he gets in a bad mood every time you pay him a compliment.

ippiki-ōkami (一匹狼) "solitary wolf" Ⓝ A lone wolf, a loner, a maverick.

あの人はどの派閥にも属さない、政界の一匹狼で有名なんだよ。

Ano hito wa dono habatsu ni mo zoku-sanai, seikai no ippiki-ōkami de yūmei nan da yo.

He's made a name for himself in political circles as a maverick because he never joined any faction.

☞ From the English "lone wolf."

iroppoi (色っぽい) "colorful" Ⓐ Sexy.

彼女は浴衣なんか着ると、妙に色っぽい。

Kanojo wa yukata nanka kiru to, myō ni iroppoi.

There's something about the way she looks in a yukata that's a real turn-on.

☞ Usually about a woman's appearance, voice, etc.

kakedashi (駆け出し) "beginning to run" N A novice, greenhorn, freshman.

浩君は去年出版社に入社したばかりの、駆け出しの編集者だわ。

Hiroshi-kun wa kyonen shuppan-sha ni nyūsha shita bakari no, kake-dashi no henshū-sha da wa.

Hiroshi's learning the ropes to be an editor. He just started working at a publishing house last year.

kamatoto (かまとと) N A (usually) young woman who feigns in-nocence about the facts of life.

あの女の子、夜遊びばかりしてるくせに会社ではカマトトなの。

Ano onna no ko, yo-asobi bakari shite 'ru kuse ni kaisha de wa kamatoto na no.

She may play the innocent at the office, but I know for a fact that she paints the town every chance she gets.

☞ Said to have originated when a woman asked if *kamaboko* or "fish paste" was made from fish, using baby talk, *toto*, for fish. Formerly the argot of the red-light district.

kechi (けち) "inauspicious" A N

1. Stingy, tight, tight-fisted, cheap; a scrooge, tightwad.

ケチ！新婚旅行のホテルまで料金の安いところにしたいわけね。

Kechi! Shinkon-ryokō no hoteru made ryōkin no yasui tokoro ni shitai wake ne.

So you want to spend our honeymoon in a cheap hotel, huh? Last of the big-time spenders!

2. Petty, small, mean, narrow-minded; a petty person.

いつまでもふられた女のことを考えてるなんて、ケチな男だな。

Itsu made mo furareta onna no koto o kangaete 'ru nante, kechi na otoko da na.

He's got to be small-minded to still be carrying the torch for some gal who gave him his walking papers.

☞ See also *sekoi*.

kireru (切れる) "to be able to cut" V Be sharp, quick-witted, on the ball.

彼の説得力にまけたよ。あんなに切れる男とは思わなかった。

Kare no settoku-ryoku ni maketa yo. Anna ni kireru otoko to wa omowanakatta.

Guy's really convincing. I didn't think he had that much on the ball.

☞ See also *surudoi*.

kiza (キザ) "a crimp on the spirits" A N Affected, pretentious; a snob.

あの男キザでさ、スーツはアルマーニだよなんて気取ってるの。

Ano otoko kiza de sa, sūtsu wa Arumāni da yo nante kidotte 'ru no.

That guy must think his shit doesn't stink the way he was bragging about having an Armani suit on and all.

☞ An abbreviation of *ki-zawari* (気障; hindrance to the spirits; i.e., a worry, an eyesore). Most often used of men.

mazakon (マザコン) N A mama's boy, someone with a mother complex.

あいつ、結婚しても毎晩母親に電話するようなマザコンなのよ。

Aitsu, kekkon shite mo maiban haha-oya ni denwa suru yō na maza-kon na no yo.

He still calls his mother every night even though he's married. What a mama's boy!

☞ Abbreviation of the English "mother complex."

menkui (面食い) "face eating" N A person who goes for good-looking women (handsome men).

おれって面食いだから、美人以外には関心ないんだ。ごめんね。

Ore tte menkui da kara, bijin igai ni wa kanshin nai n' da. Gomen ne.

Sorry, Babe, but I only go for the lookers, and, well, that leaves you out.

☞ Originally used about women who worked in bars and slept with any man as long as he was handsome.

mīhā (ミーハー) A N A bimbo, bubblehead, airhead.

マイケルのためなら死んでもいいなんて、ミーハーなやつだね。

Maikeru no tame nara shinde mo ii nante, mīhā na yatsu da ne.

Image some skirt carrying on about how she'd die for a cartoon cat named Michael! What a bimbo!

ルイ・ビトンのバッグを欲しがるのは、ミーハーギャルだけだ。

Rui-Biton no baggu o hoshigaru no wa, mīhā-gyaru dake da.

Only a Heather would want a Louis Vuitton bag.

☞ Abbreviation of Mīchan-Hāchan (origin unclear), a derogatory reference to young people, especially girls who are thought to have bad taste and minimal education.

moteru (モテる) "to be able to carry" V Be popular (with the opposite sex), have to beat the men (women) off with a stick.

雅史はハンサムで背が高いから、学校でもよくモテるだろうね。

Masashi wa hansamu de se ga takai kara, gakkō de mo yoku moteru darō ne.

Masashi's tall and handsome, so I bet he's got lots of girls chasing him at school.

neaka (ネアカ) "bright root" N Cheerful, happy-go-lucky, bright.

イギリス人のポールはネアカで、人を笑わせるのが得意なのよ。

Igirisu-jin no Pōru wa neaka de, hito o warawaseru no ga tokui na no yo.

That Englishman Paul is basically a cheerful kind of guy with a knack for making people laugh.

☞ Shortened form of *nekkara akarui* (根っから明るい). *Neaka* entered the language as the opposite of *nekura* (see following).

nekura (ネクラ) "dark root" N A stick in the mud, a wet blanket, a killjoy, a gloomy Gus.

花子、哲学書なんか読んでると ネクラと思われるわ。

Hanako, tetsugaku-sho nanka yonde 'ru to nekura to omowareru wa.

Hey, Hanako, people are going to think you're one of those gloomy types if you insist on reading philosophy books.

☞ Shortened form of *ne ga kurai*, in which *ne* ("root") means disposition or nature. Since 1982.

nonbē (飲ん兵衛) "drinking Bei" N A heavy drinker, guzzler.

叔父さんは飲んべえだから、酒さえあればニコニコしてるのさ。

Oji-san wa nonbē da kara, sake sae areba nikoniko shite 'ru no sa.

Boozer that he is, my uncle's happy as a clam as long as there's some juice around.

☞ *Bē* derives from two characters (兵衛; *hē*) formerly appended to masculine given names.

nōtarin (脳足りん) "short-of-brains" N Birdbrain, dimwit, numbskull.

あんた脳足りんねえ。洗濯機に洗剤入れないで洗うつもりなの？

Anta nōtarin nē. Sentaku-ki ni senzai irenai de arau tsumori na no?

Hey, dummy, you're not going to try to wash clothes without any laundry soap, are you?

☞ See also *aho*, *baka*, *pā*, and *teinō*.

nōtenki (脳(能)天気) "fair-weather brain" N Recklessness, rashness; a cowboy. A Foolhardy, reckless.

お金もないのにイタリアに行こうなんて、脳天気な人だわ。

Okane mo nai no ni Itaria ni ikō nante, nōtenki na hito da wa.

What a cowboy! Talking about taking off for Italy without any money.

omedetai (おめでたい) "happy" A Naive, wide-eyed, like a babe in the woods, honest to a fault.

自分をだました詐欺師に同情を感じるとは、おめでたいやつだね。

Jibun o damashita sagi-shi ni dōjō o kanjiru to wa, omedetai yatsu da ne.

Guy's gotta be a real Bambi to feel sorry for the con man that fleeced him.

onchi (音痴) "sound silly" N

1. Tone deafness; a tone-deaf person.

きみがカラオケが好きなのは仕方がないけど、音痴なのは許せない。

Kimi ga karaoke ga suki na no wa shikata ga nai kedo, onchi na no wa yurusenai.

I guess it's our tough luck that you like karaoke, but you've got to do something about that tin ear of yours.

2. [As a suffix] inability to do a certain thing; such a person.

ぼくは方向音痴で、地図を見てもいつも道に迷ってしまうんだ。

Boku wa hōkō-onchi de, chizu o mite mo itsumo michi ni mayotte shimau n' da.

I just have no sense of direction. Even with a map, I get lost all the time.

onna-tarashi (女たらし) "woman wheedler" N A wolf, lady-killer, womanizer, stud, hound dog, tomcat, Romeo, smooth operator.

あいつは女たらしで、何人の女を泣かせてきたかわからないぞ。

Aitsu wa onna-tarashi de, nannin no onna o nakasete kita ka wakaranai zo.

He's a love 'em and leave 'em kinda guy. No telling how many hearts he's broken.

☞ *Tarashi* (from *tarasu*) here means to sweet talk or soft soap an adult or child.

osenchi (おセンチ) A [Female usage] sentimental, teary-eyed.

海岸でひとり夕日を見てたら、ちょっとおセンチになったわ。

Kaigan de hitori yūhi o mite 'tara, chotto osenchi ni natta wa.

I got a little lump in my throat watching the sun set all alone at the beach.

☞ *Senchi* is a shortened form of English "sentimental." *O* is the polite prefix.

oshama (おしゃま) N [Of young girls] precociousness, precocity; a precocious girl. A Precocious, grown-up for one's age.

姪っこはまだ5歳なのにおしゃまで、お化粧に興味を持ってる。

Meikko wa mada gosai na no ni oshama de, okeshō ni kyōmi o motte 'ru.

My niece is quite the little lady. She's only five and already showing an interest in makeup.

otchokochoi (おっちょこちょい) "flibbertigibbet" Ⓐ Addle-brained, flighty, scatterbrained. Ⓝ A dingbat, ding-a-ling, yo-yo, squirrel, scatterbrain.

うちの主人はおっちょこちょいで、いつも傘を電車に忘れてくるのよ。

Uchi no shujin wa otchokochoi de, itsumo kasa o densha ni wasurete kuru no yo.

My rattlebrained husband's always going off and forgetting his umbrella in the train.

☞ Probably associated with *chokochoko* (fidget).

otenkiya (お天気屋) "weather man/woman" Ⓝ A fickled person, a temperamental person, someone who blows hot and cold.

彼女はお天気屋だから、ぼくはデートのたびにふりまわされる。

Kanojo wa otenkiya da kara, boku wa dēto no tabi ni furimawa-sareru.

She's so moody that I can't keep track of which way is up when we're out on a date.

oya-baka (親馬鹿) "parents' stupidity" Ⓝ A doting parent; blind parental love.

後藤さんはいつも自分の息子の自慢話ばかりで、親馬鹿なんだ。

Gotō-san wa itsumo jibun no musuko no jiman-banashi bakari de, oya-baka nan da.

That Goto is a doting father if there ever was one. All he ever does is go on and on about his son.

pā (パー) "ding-a-ling" Ⓝ Stupid, dumb, dim, a few bricks short of a load, dense; a lamebrain, idiot, squirrel.

おまえパーかよ、こんな単純な計算も電卓でなきゃ無理なのか？

Omae pā ka yo, konna tanjun na keisan mo dentaku de nakya muri na no ka?

Come on, dufus, don't tell me you can't even handle simple arithmetic without a calculator?

☞ See also *aho, baka, nōtarin,* and *teinō.*

pika-ichi (ピカイチ) "first sparkler" Ⓝ [Usually of people] head and shoulders above the rest, the cream of the crop.

ルックスじゃ、あんたがこの店じゃピカイチだって評判だぜ。

Rukkusu ja, anta ga kono mise ja pika-ichi datte hyōban da ze.

Everybody says you're the most outa sight chick working here. / Word is that there's no other girl here who can hold a candle to you in the looks department.

☞ From the traditional card game of *hanafuda* in which only one of the seven cards in a hand is of value. The valuable card is called *hikari-mono,* or "the one that shines." *Pika* is the mimetic word used to express sparkling or twinkling.

sabaketa (さばけた) **"untangled"** Ⓐ Together, laid-back, down-home, down-to-earth, up-front, cool.

おれのダチはさばけたやつだから、なんでも正直に言っていい。

Ore no dachi wa sabaketa yatsu da kara, nan de mo shōjiki ni itte ii.

My buddy's shit's together, man, so just tell it like it is.

sekoi (せこい) **"poor (house)"** Ⓐ Tight, stingy, tightfisted.

おまえせこいね。辞書ぐらい、人のを借りずに自分のを買えよ！

Omae sekoi ne. Jisho gurai, hito no o karizu ni jibun no o kae yo!

Hey, your middle name tight, or what? Get your own damn dictionary and stop moochin' mine!
☞ Formerly used by actors and vaudevillians about a poor audience. See also *kechi*.

shibui (シブイ／渋い) **"tangy"** Ⓐ Heavy, cool, mellow.

あいつは無口でカッコよくて責任感があって、本当にシブイよな。

Aitsu wa mukuchi de kakko yokute sekinin-kan ga atte, hontō ni shibui yo na.

The guy's one cool dude; doesn't talk much, looks sharp, and can handle responsibility.

shirigaru (尻軽) **"light butt"** Ⓐ Ⓝ (Female) promiscuity, sleeping around.

声をかけられると、だれにでもほいほいついていく。尻軽女め！

Koe o kakerareru to, dare ni de mo hoihoi tsuite iku. Shirigaru onna-me!

You slut! You'd jump into bed with any guy that hits on you.

sukebē (助平) **"lech"** Ⓐ Lecherous, horny, raunchy. Ⓝ A lecher, lech, dirty old man.

あいつ、けっこう助平だぜ。毎晩エロビデオ観てるって噂だよ。

Aitsu, kekkō sukebē da ze. Maiban ero-bideo mite 'ru tte uwasa da yo.

He's a horny mother, alright. Word is that he watches dirty videos every night.

増田の野郎、助平根性だして隣の女子寮を覗くのに一生懸命だ。

Masuda no yarō, sukebē-konjō dashite tonari no joshi-ryō o nozoku no ni isshō-kenmei da.

Fuckin' Masuda's practically slobbering all over himself trying to get a peek into the girl's dorm next door.

助平じじい、あたしのお尻がそんなに触りたいの。絶対いやよ。

Sukebē-jijī, atashi no oshiri ga sonna ni sawaritai no. Zettai iya yo.

What do you think you're doing, trying to touch my butt, you dirty old man? No way!

☞ A combination of *suke* (derived from *suki*, "to like") and *bē*, a common appendage to masculine names. See also *etchi*.

surudoi (鋭い) "sharp" Ⓐ Quick, sharp, on the ball.

絵を見ただけでカレル・アペルのだってわかるとは、鋭いねえ。

E o mita dake de Kareru Aperu no datte wakaru to wa, surudoi nē.

That's quite an eye you've got there, being able to tell a Karl Appel on sight.

☞ See also *kireru*.

teinō (低能) "shallow talent" Ⓐ Dumb, slow-witted, thick, have an air-temperature I.Q. Ⓝ A no-neck, dolt, butthead, dumbfuck.

ＣＤの扱い方もわからないなんて、おまえも低能なやつだな。

Shīdī no atsukai-kata mo wakaranai nante, omae mo teinō na yatsu da na.

You don't even know what to do with a CD? Where were you when the brains were passed out?

☞ Originally an abbreviation for *teinō-ji* (低能児; mentally retarded child), and to be absolutely avoided in that sense. See also *aho*, *baka*, *nōtarin*, and *pā*.

toroi (とろい) "low-flamed" Ⓐ Slow, stupid, dumb, dumb as a box of rocks.

あんた、本当にとろいわね。ワープロの使い方、昨日教えたじゃない。

Anta, hontō ni toroi wa ne. Wāpuro no tsukai-kata, kinō oshieta ja nai.

You're such a bonehead! Didn't I just show you yesterday how to use that word processor?

☞ See also *donkan*.

tsuppari (ツッパリ) "thrusting away" Ⓝ Rebelliousness; a rebellious boy (girl), juvenile delinquent, juvie, punk.

親に反抗してツッパリになっても、親の愛情は十分感じてるさ。

Oya ni hankō shite tsuppari ni natte mo, oya no aijō wa jūbun kanjite 'ru sa.

Kids who rebel against their parents still know that they're loved.

ツッパリは、世間につっぱることで自己主張してるんだ。

Tsuppari wa, seken ni tsupparu koto de jiko-shuchō shite 'ru n' da.

Juvies are just trying to express themselves by taking on the world.

☞ Since 1975.

yancha (やんちゃ) Ⓐ Mischievous, naughty. Ⓝ A holy terror, little monkey, little dickens, urchin.

弟はとてもやんちゃで、わたしの言うことなんか聞きもしない。

The Body and Its Functions:
Surprised Eyes and a Pekinese Sneeze

bero (ベロ／べろ) Ⓝ Tongue.

女の子がベロを出したりするのは、とてもはしたないことだよ。

Onna no ko ga bero o dashitari suru no wa, totemo hashitanai koto da yo.

It's really gross for a girl to stick her tongue out like that.

☞ The ordinary word for tongue is *shita* (舌). An interesting but undoubtedly unrelated fact: *bero* is the word for cow in the Tohoku dialect.

bikkuri-manako (びっくりまなこ／びっくり眼) "surprised eyes" Ⓝ Banjo eyes, saucer eyes.

突然帰ってきたぼくを見て、母さんはびっくりまなこになった。

Totsuzen kaette kita boku o mite, kāsan wa bikkuri-manako ni natta.

You should'a seen the look on my mother's face when I showed up.

boin (ボイン) "boobs" Ⓝ Knockers, built, stacked, built like a brick shithouse.

姉貴は細身だけどボインで、出るとこはしっかり出てるんだ。

Aneki wa hosomi da kedo boin de, deru toko wa shikkari dete 'ru n' da.

My big sister may be skinny, but she's built. Got some big hooters.

そこのボインちゃん、おれにもビール１本もってきてくれない？

Soko no boin-chan, ore ni mo bīru ippon motte kite kurenai?

Hey, Chesty. How about bringin' me a beer, too?

buta (ブタ) "pig" Ⓝ A pig, lard-ass, porker; [of a woman] a cow, heifer.

香港でごちそうばかり食べていたら、いっぺんでブタになったわ。

Honkon de gochisō bakari tabete itara, ippen de buta ni natta wa.

I stuffed my face while I was in Hong Kong and ballooned right out before I knew it.

☞ Pejorative.

chibi (チビ) "stub" Ⓐ Short. Ⓝ Half-pint, midget, runt, shrimp, squirt.

背が低いからって、チビって呼ぶなら、おまえとは絶交するぜ。

Se ga hikui kara tte, chibe tte yobu nara, omae to wa zekkō suru ze.

I'm gonna stop hanging out with you if you keep callin' me a pip-squeak just because I'm short.

☞ Pejorative. The name *chibi* is often given to cute little puppies etc., who often grow up to be Great Danes etc.

chinchin (チンチン) "teeny-weeny" Ⓝ Pee-pee, peter, weenie.

あの男の子、小さなチンチンまる出しで公園を走り回ってらあ。

Ano otoko no ko, chiisa na chinchin marudashi de kōen o hashiri-mawatterā.

Look at that kid out there running around the park with his little peter swinging in the wind.

☞ Diminutive. Used primarily of a child's penis. Honorifically, *ochinchin*. Other less widely used terms include *chinbo* and *chinpo*.

chinkusha (ちんくしゃ) "Pekinese sneeze" Ⓝ A skank, sweat hog, two-bagger, piss-ugly.

あいつの彼女、顔はちんくしゃだけど性格はとてもいい子でかわいいんだ。

Aitsu no kanojo, kao wa chinkusha da kedo seikaku wa totemo ii ko de kawaii n' da.

Dude's girlfriend may be a skag, but she's a little sweetheart.

☞ Pejorative. Portmanteau formed from *chin* (狆), a Pekinese dog, and *kusha*, shortened from *kushami*, a sneeze. Hence, a face so ugly that it resembles a Pekinese sneezing.

daikon-ashi (大根足) "daikon legs" Ⓝ Fat legs.

大根足だから、白いストッキングはやめといたほうがいいわね。

Daikon-ashi da kara, shiroi sutokkingu wa yametoita hō ga ii wa ne.

I guess I'd better stay away from white stockings with these stubby legs of mine.

☞ Pejorative.

dangoppana (団子っ鼻) "dumpling nose" Ⓝ A bulbous (snub, squat) nose.

ぼくの団子っ鼻には、どんなサングラスも似合わないんだなあ。

Boku no dangoppana ni wa, donna sangurasu mo niawanai n' da nā.

What a bummer. No way I'll ever find a pair of sunglasses that'll look good on a schnozz like mine.

debu (デブ) "fatty" Ⓐ Fat, chunky, roly-poly, tubby, pudgy. Ⓝ Fatso, fat slob, tub of lard, lard-ass, porker.

デブ！食ってばかりで運動しないから、どんどん太るんだぞ。

Debu! Kutte bakari de undō shinai kara, dondon futoru n' da zo.

No wonder you're porking out, Fatso. All you do is feed your face and never get any exercise.
☞ Pejorative.

deppa (出っ歯) **"outgoing teeth"** Ⓝ Buckteeth; [the person] Bucky, Bucky Beaver.

自分の出っ歯がそんなに嫌なら、歯医者で矯正すればいいのに。

Jibun no deppa ga sonna ni iya nara, ha-isha de kyōsei sureba ii no ni.

If your buckteeth bother you that much, why don't you just go to the dentist and get 'em fixed.

era (エラ) **"gills"** Ⓝ Jaw, jawbone.

松田君はエラが張ってるから、爬虫類みたいって言われるんだ。

Matsuda-kun wa era ga hatte 'ru kara, hachū-rui mitai tte iwareru n' da.

Everybody says Matsuda looks like a reptile because his jawbone sticks out on the sides.

gachame (ガチャメ／がちゃ目) **"muddled eye(s)"** Ⓝ Blind in one eye; someone with one blind eye; someone who is cockeyed.

あの先公はガチャメで、こっちを見てんのか見てないのかわからねえ。

Ano senkō wa gachame de, kotchi o miten no ka mite nai no ka wakaranē.

That damn teacher's so cockeyed you never know whether he's looking at you or not.
☞ Pejorative. *Gacha* possibly comes from *gachagacha* (disorderly, messy).

gankubi (雁首) **"goose neck"** Ⓝ Ugly puss, mug.

今そっちへ行くからな。貴様ら雁首並べて待っていやがれ！

Ima sotchi e iku kara na. Kisama-ra gankubi narabete matte iyagare!

I'm on my way now, so you ugly fuckers better be ready when I get there.
☞ Slightly pejorative.

garigari (ガリガリ) **"scraggy"** Ⓐ Skinny, skin and bones, bony, scrawny. Ⓝ A bag of bones, a skeleton.

拒食症になった人って、みんなガリガリにやせてしまうのよね。

Kyoshoku-shō ni natta hito tte, minna garigari ni yasete shimau no yo ne.

I guess anorectic people just end up all skin and bones.

gejigeji-mayuge (ゲジゲジ眉毛) **"centipede eyebrows"** Ⓝ Bushy eyebrows.

あんちゃんは、ゲジゲジ眉毛を床屋で細く剃ってもらったんだ。

Anchan wa, gejigeji-mayuge o tokoya de hosoku sotte moratta n' da.

My big brother had the barber trim those big, bushy eyebrows of his.

gero (ゲロ) **"glob"** N Barf, liquid laugh, puke, vomit.

おれ昨日は飲みすぎて、地下鉄のホームでゲロ吐いちゃったよ。

Ore kinō wa nómisugite, chikatestu no hōmu de gero haichatta yo.

I got so smashed yesterday that I ended up ralphing (heaving, blowing chunks) all over the subway platform.

☞ Origin unclear.

gitcho (ぎっちょ) **"skilly"** N A lefty, southpaw, someone left-handed.

あたしは、食べるときだけぎっちょになるの。ほかのときは右よ。

Atashi wa, taberu toki dake gitcho ni naru no. Hoka no toki wa migi yo.

I eat left-handed but do everything else with my right hand.

☞ While the derivation of *gitcho* is far from clear, one suggested possibility is a corrupted abbreviation of *hidari-kiyō* (ひだり器用; skilled with the left [hand]).

harapeko (腹ぺこ) **"sunken stomach"** A N Starving, starved, dying of hunger, could eat a horse.

朝から何も食べていないから、ぼくもう腹ぺこで倒れそうなんだ。

Asa kara nani mo tabete inai kara, boku mō harapeko de taoresō nan da.

I haven't had anything to eat since breakfast, so I'm starving to death.

☞ Shortened from *hara ga pekopeko* (famished), *pekopeko* originally meant a depression, sunken area, or dent made by an object's being poked or pushed.

hecha (へちゃ) **"funny"** A Pug-nosed; a face that only a mother could love, plug-ugly.

あんたのようなヘチャな顔は、整形外科でも手術は難しいのよ。

Anta no yō na hecha na kao wa, seikei-geka de mo shujutsu wa muzukashii no yo.

Even with some plastic surgery it wouldn't be easy to fix up a ugly-duckling face like yours.

☞ The origin of the word is unclear.

inpo (インポ) N Impotence; a limp-shrimp, half-master, can't get it up; wimp.

女が怖いだなんて、このインポ！情けないこと言うんじゃない！

Onna ga kowai da nante, kono inpo! Nasakenai koto iu n' ja nai!

Say what? You're afraid of girls? Quit your whining, you limp-dick.
☞ From German "Impotenz."

katawa (かたわ) **"one-sided"** Ⓝ A cripple, crip, gimp.

工場で働いていたとき、機械に手を挟まれてカタワになった。

Kōjo de hataraite ita toki, kikai ni te o hasamarete katawa ni natta.

I crippled myself up when I got my hand caught in a machine at the
   factory where I was working.
☞ Scornful. The kanji are 片端.

ketsu (ケツ／穴) **"hole"** Ⓝ Butt, booty, can, tail, cheeks, buns,
duff.

サイクリングで遠出して50キロも走ったから、ケツが痛いよ。

Saikuringu de tōde-shite gojukkiro mo hashitta kara, ketsu ga itai yo.

Fifty kilos on the bicycle, and boy does my ass hurt.
☞ Vulgar.

kintama (キンタマ／金玉) **"golden balls"** Ⓝ Balls, nuts, nads,
cajones, family jewels.

キンタマついてるだろ？男ならもっと堂々としたらどうだい。

Kintama tsuite 'ru daro? Otoko nara motto dōdō to shitara dō dai.

You got balls, or what? Don't act like such a wimp!
☞ Vulgar.

mentama (めん玉) **"eyeball"** Ⓝ Eyeball, headlight(s).

きのう食べた寿司屋はなかなかうまかったけど、めん玉が飛び出るほ
   ど高かった。

*Kinō tabeta sushi-ya wa nakanaka umakatta kedo, mentama ga tobi-
   deru hodo takakatta.*

The sushi shop I ate at yesterday was pretty good, but my eyes nearly
   popped out of my head when I saw the bill.

ちくしょう！今度あいつを見つけたら、めん玉くり抜いてやる。

Chikushō! Kondo aitsu o mitsuketara, mentama kurinuite yaru.

I'm gonna rip that fucker's eyeballs out when I find him.
☞ Vulgar.

misoppa (みそっ歯) **"bean-paste teeth"** Ⓝ Rotten teeth.

うちの子供は甘いものの食べすぎで、みそっ歯になってしまった。

*Uchi no kodomo wa amai mono no tabesugi de, misoppa ni natte shi-
   matta.*

My daughter has bad teeth from eating so many sweets.

☞ From *miso* (味噌), a word affixed to others to convey a sense of derision or scorn, and *ha*.

mutchiri (むっちり) "resilient" Ⓐ Tight, firm, hard-bodied.

あの女のむっちりしたお尻は、はっきり言って一種の犯罪だね。

Ano onna no mutchiri shita oshiri wa, hakkiri itte isshu no hanzai da ne.

There ought'a be a law against booties (an ass) like the one that little hardbody is packin'. / A tight ass like that gal's ought'a be a crime.

☞ In standard usage, *mutchiri* refers to a well-muscled, supple physique, as in *mutchiri (to) shita karada-tsuki*.

nodochinko (ノドチンコ／喉ちんこ) "throat penis" Ⓝ Uvula.

気管支炎のせいで、ノドチンコが真っ赤に腫れあがってるんだ。

Kikanshi-en no sei de, nodochinko ga makka ni hareagatte 'ru n' da.

My uvula (throat) is all red and swollen from having bronchitis.

☞ The standard term is *kōgai-sui* (口蓋垂).

noppo (ノッポ) "towering"

1. [Of a person] Ⓐ Tall and skinny, twiggy. Ⓝ A beanstalk, bean pole, broomstick, stringbean.

あんまりチビも嫌だけど、ノッポも好きにはなれないよね。

Anmari chibi mo iya da kedo, noppo mo suki ni wa narenai yo ne.

I don't want someone who's too short, but I can't get excited about beanstalks either.

2. [Of a building] Ⓐ Tall. Ⓝ A skyscraper.

新宿はノッポのビルが林立してるから、ニューヨークみたいね。

Shinjuku wa noppo no biru ga rinritsu shite 'ru kara, Nyūyōku mitai ne.

Shinjuku's beginning to look like New York, what with tall buildings sprouting up everywhere.

☞ Probably associated with *noppori*, the primary meaning of which is "exceedingly tall."

ochobo-guchi (おちょぼ口) "petite mouth" Ⓝ Little pursed lips; a cute little mouth.

あんたいつも大口開けて食べるのに、彼の前ではおちょぼ口ね。

Anta itsumo ōguchi akete taberu no ni, kare no mae de wa ochobo-guchi ne.

Why do you always purse your lips like Miss Manners when he's around, but shovel down the food when he's not?

☞ *Chobo* originally meant "small," while an *ochobo* was a young girl in her early teens who worked as an assistant in a red-light district.

omeme (おめめ／お目目) (eye eye) N Eye.

太郎ちゃん、おめめがかゆくても擦ってはだめよ。目薬あげるわ。

Tarō-chan, omeme ga kayukute mo kosutte wa dame yo. Megusuri ageru wa.

Now Taro, don't rub your eye even if it itches. Mommy will give you some eye drops in a minute.

☞ Baby talk.

oppai (オッパイ) N

1. Mother's milk.

ママ、ミルクはね、牛のオッパイだって先生が教えてくれたよ。

Mama, miruku wa ne, ushi no oppai datte sensei ga oshiete kureta yo.

Mommy, the teacher told us that milk comes from cows. / Mommy, the teacher told us that cow's milk is the same as mommy's milk.

☞ Baby talk.

2. Breast, titty, tit, boob, hooter.

姉貴のオッパイはでっかくて、すごいボインでセクシーなんだ。

Aneki no oppai wa dekkakute, sugoi boin de sekushī nan da.

My big sister's so stacked, she's really sexy.

pechapai (ペチャパイ) "flat breasts" N Flat-chested, little tits, small breasts.

あたしみたいなペチャパイには、ブラジャーなんか要らないの。

Atashi mitai na pechapai ni wa, burajā nanka iranai no.

I'm so flat-chested that I don't need to wear a bra.

☞ *Pecha* is a shortened form of *pechanko* (flat), and *pai* is *oppai* (breasts).

ronpari (ロンパリ) "Lon[don]–Paris" N Walleye, walleyes, a walleyed person.

ロンパリの目つきの女はセックスアピールがあるって本当かな。

Ronpari no me-tsuki no onna wa sekkusu-apīru ga aru tte hontō ka na.

I wonder if what they say about walleyed (cockeyed) women having a lot of sex appeal is really true.

☞ From the notion that those afflicted with such a vision abnormality can look toward London with one eye and Paris with the other. Pejorative.

shonben (しょんべん) "small excrement" N Piss, pee.

ちょっと待っててくれる？あそこでしょんべんしてくるからさ。

Chotto matte 'te kureru? Asoko de shonben shite kuru kara sa.

Wait up. I'm gonna take a leak (make a pit stop / see a man about a dog) over there.

☞ Vulgar male usage. A variation of *shōben* (小便; urine).

suppin (すっぴん) **"bare-faced"** Ⓝ A face without makeup.

化粧してるときもいいけど、すっぴんの彼女はもっとすてきだ。

Keshō shite 'ru toki mo ii kedo, suppin no kanojo wa motto suteki da.

She looks good enough with makeup on, but she's a 10 (a real knockout) without it.

☞ Formed from *su* (素), a character meaning "natural" or without adornment, and *pin*, a slang term for "face."

tako-nyūdō (タコ入道) **"octopus monk"** Ⓝ Baldy, cue ball.

あのタコ入道、怒ると真っ赤になって、本当にタコそっくりだ。

Ano tako-nyūdō, okoru to makka ni natte, hontō ni tako sokkuri da.

When old baldy gets pissed off, he turns red as beet and looks just like a boiled octopus.

☞ From the fact that both octopi and sheared monks have hairless heads.

tankobu (たんこぶ／たん瘤) Ⓝ A bump, lump, knot.

柱にぶつけて頭にでっかいたんこぶができちゃった。冷やそう。

Hashira ni butsukete atama ni dekkai tankobu ga dekichatta. Hiyasō.

I ran into a post and got a huge bump on my head. I'm gonna put some ice on it.

☞ The standard word is simply *kobu*.

tansoku (短足) **"short legs"** Ⓝ Short legs; a groundhog, squatty-body.

サッカー選手のおれにとって、短足がいちばんの悩みの種だね。

Sakkā-senshu no ore ni totte, tansoku ga ichiban no nayami no tane da ne.

Built close to the ground the way I am makes it hard for me to be the soccer player I know I can be. / For a soccer player like me, it's really tough being built so close to the ground.

tenpā (天パー) Ⓝ Naturally curly (frizzy, kinky) hair.

ぼくはパーマなんてかけてないですよ。天パーなんです。

Boku wa pāma nante kakete 'nai desu yo. Tenpā nan desu.

Hey, man, this isn't a permanent. This is the way I was born.

☞ Shortened form of *tennen pāma* (天然パーマ), or "natural permanent." Current among young people.

tsura つら (ツラ／面) **"phiz"** Ⓝ Mug, puss.

おまえのツラは二度と見たくねえや。とっととどっかに消えろ！

Omae no tsura wa nido to mitaku nee ya. Totto to dokka ni kiero!

I don't ever want to see your ugly puss around here again. Now get out'a my sight while the gettin's good.

☞ Male usage.

tsuruppage (つるっぱげ／つるっ禿) "slippery bald" N Complete baldness, smooth as a baby's ass; cueball, skinhead, baldy.

隣りのおじさんはつるっぱげで、ハエもすべって落ちると思うな。

Tonari no oji-san wa tsuruppage de, hae mo subette ochiru to omou na.

The old guy next door's head is so bald that I'll bet that even a fly'd have trouble getting a foothold.

wakahage (若ハゲ) "young and bald" N Premature baldness; a person bald before his time.

山本くんはまだ22歳なのに、若ハゲのせいでおじんに見えるわ。

Yamamoto-kun wa mada nijūni-sai na no ni, wakahage no sei de ojin ni mieru wa.

Poor Yamamoto, only 22 and bald already. He looks like an old man.

yorime (ヨリ目／寄り目) "converging eyes" N Cross-eyed; a cross-eyed person.

じーっとてんとう虫を見てたら、目がヨリ目になっちゃったよ。

Jitto tentō-mushi o mite 'tara, me ga yorime ni natchatta yo.

I went cross-eyed from staring too long at a ladybug.

zūtai (図体) "trunk" N [Especially big or well-built] body, bod.

アメフトの選手は図体がでかくて、怪物みたいな男が多いわ。

Amefuto no senshu wa zūtai ga dekakute, kaibutsu mitai na otoko ga ōi wa.

Most football players are big, brawny (studly) guys—regular monsters.

☞ According to one theory, a variant pronunciation of the standard 胴体 (*dōtai*), with approximately the same meaning.

Action and Change:
Dismantling, Cooking, and Tinkling

akappaji o kaku (赤っ恥をかく) "be embarrassed red" Ⅴ Feel so stupid, have egg on one's face, be red-faced, be so embarrassed.

プールに飛び込んだらパンツが脱げちゃって赤っ恥をかいたよ。

Pūru ni tobikondara pantsu ga nugechatte akappaji o kaita yo.

I could have died when I dived into the pool and my trunks came off.
☞ Emphatic form of *haji o kaku*.

amattareru (甘ったれる) "be sweetened" Ⅴ [Especially of children] be super dependent, be a momma's boy; [of an adult] be tied to one's mother's apron strings; rely (lean) on.

甘ったれるな！自分の不始末は自分で解決しなくちゃだめだぞ。

Amattareru na! Jibun no fu-shimatsu wa jibun de kaiketsu shinakucha dame da zo.

Don't look at me! You gotta learn that if you screw up, it's nobody's fault but your own (that when you mess up, you have to clean up after yourself).
☞ Colloquial variation of *amatareru*.

baito (バイト) Ｎ A part-time job, gig. Ⅴ (*suru*) Work.

おれは家庭教師のバイトで学費をかせいでいるから忙しいんだ。

Ore wa katei-kyōshi no baito de gakuhi o kaseide iru kara isogashii n' da.

Working my way through college as a part-time tutor keeps me busy.
☞ Shortened form of German "Arbeit." The standard form is *arubaito*.

barasu (ばらす) "to take apart, dismantle" Ⅴ

1. Expose, tell everyone, let the cat out of the bag, spill the beans.

お金を払わないなら、あんたの秘密を会社にばらすぞ。

Okane o harawanai nara, anta no himitsu o kaisha ni barasu zo.

If you don't want me to let everyone at the office know what you've been up to, you'd better pay up.

2. Kill, waste, off, chill, snuff, rub out, wax.

あいつの口をふさぐには、ばらす以外にない。

Aitsu no kuchi o fusagu ni wa, barasu igai ni nai.

We're gonna have to waste that dude to shut him up.

bateru (ばてる) **"be done in"** Ⅴ Be bushed, wiped out, worn out, fagged, pooped, dog tired, draggin' ass.

この猛暑で、すっかりばてたわ。夏バテ解消法を何か知らない？

Kono mōsho de, sukkari bateta wa. Natsu-bate kaishō-hō o nani ka shiranai?

This heat wave is about to do me in. Any ideas about how to beat the heat?

☞ Thought to be a corruption of *hateru* (to conclude, do something to an extreme, expire). In horse racing *bateru* refers to horses that get off to a good start but peter out at the wire. See also *hebaru*.

benkyō suru (勉強する) **"to study"** Ⅴ Discount, give someone something off.

定価25万円のエアコンを、勉強して19万円でいかがでしょう。

Teika nijūgo-man'en no eakon o, benkyō shite jūkyū-man'en de ikaga deshō.

What would you say to one hundred ninety thousand yen for an air-conditioner that lists for two fifty? / I'll tell you what I'm gonna do. I'll let you have it for one ninety even though it lists for two fifty.

☞ Used by retailers.

betabeta suru (べたべたする) **"to be sticky"** Ⅴ Flirt, come on to, make bedroom eyes at; make out, pet, fool around with, play touchy-feely, go to town.

あいつはかわいい子を見つけると、近づいてすぐベタベタするんだ。

Aitsu wa kawaii ko o mitsukeru to, chikazuite sugu betabeta suru n' da.

Guy tries to hit on (starts making up to) any good-looking chick he runs across.

電車の中で若いカップルがベタベタしてるのはうっとうしいね。

Densha no naka de wakai kappuru ga betabeta shite 'ru no wa uttō-shii ne.

It really gets me when I see young couples all over each other in the train.

bokeru (ぼける) **"to be addled"** Ⅴ Go senile, lose one's grip, go soft in the head.

年をとってぼけると、まるで赤ちゃんみたいになってしまう人が多いらしい。

Toshi o totte bokeru to, maru de akachan mitai ni natte shimau hito ga ōi rashii.

It seems that lots of people go into a sort of second childhood when they get old and senile.

boro-mōke (ぼろ儲け) **"clean profit"** Ⓝ Ⓥ (*suru*) Strike it rich, hit the jackpot, make money hand over fist, have a license to print money.

100円で仕入れた民芸品が1,000円で売れるなら、おれはぼろ儲けだ。

Hyaku-en de shiireta mingei-hin ga sen-en de ureru nara, ore wa boro-mōke da.

I'll make a mint if I can get a thousand yen for these handicrafts that I picked up for a hundred yen.

株の暴落でぼろ儲けする人がいるっていうのも、理不尽な話だ。

Kabu no bōraku de boro-mōke suru hito ga iru tte iu no mo, ri-fujin na hanashi da.

It blows my mind to hear about people makin' megabucks when the stock market crashes.

☞ *Boro* comes from the adjective *boroi* (very profitable; easy money). *Mōke* derives from *mōkeru* (to make a profit).

boru (ぼる) **"to cash in"** Ⓥ Rip off, take to the cleaners, gouge, stick it to one.

あのバーは、ビール1本で何千円もぼるから行っちゃだめよ。

Ano bā wa, bīru ippon de nan-zen'en mo boru kara itcha dame yo.

Better stay away from that bar. They'll stick you for thousands of yen for a measly bottle of beer.

☞ From the noun *bōri* (暴利), "outrageous profits"; originally stock market usage.

boyaku (ぼやく) **"to whine"** Ⓥ Bitch, grumble, gripe, cry.

うちの主人は、お小遣いが少ないって、ぼやいてばかりいるわ。

Uchi no shujin wa, okozukai ga sukunai tte, boyaite bakari iru wa.

All my hubby ever does is moan and groan about not having (about me not giving him) enough pocket money.

charachara suru (ちゃらちゃらする) **"to tinkle"** Ⓥ

1. [Of a woman] flirt, make eyes at, play up to.

あの子、社内の男性にチャラチャラするのはやめてもらいたいわ。

Ano ko, shanai no dansei ni charachara suru no wa yamete moraitai wa.

I just wish she'd (that little thing would) stop making eyes at every guy in the office, that's all.

2. [Of clothes or the way one dresses] flashy, trashy.

君はチャラチャラした服装より、渋めの格好のほうが似合うよ。

Kimi wa charachara shita fukusō yori, shibume no kakkō no hō ga niau yo.

You'd look better in something conservative rather than those flashy things you usually wear.

☞ Contemptuous.

chekku o ireru (チェックを入れる) "to check into" Ⓥ

1. Check, check up on.

彼の部屋へ電話でチェックを入れると、いつも女が出るの。許せない！

Kare no heya e denwa de chekku o ireru to, itsumo onna ga deru no. Yurusenai!

Every time I call to check up on him, some woman answers the phone. I've just about had it.

2. Check out (a girl), scope out.

前からチェックを入れてたかわいい子がうちのクラブに入ったんだ。

Mae kara chekku o irete 'ta kawaii ko ga uchi no kurabu ni haitta n' da.

That cute little chick that I've had my eye on (had the hots for) joined the same club I'm in.

☞ From the English "check." Youth.

chibiru (ちびる) "to do something a little at a time" Ⓥ

1. Pee (wet) one's pants, shit one's pants.

ジェットコースターの勢いで、弟のやつおしっこちびったんだ。

Jetto-kōsutā no ikioi de, otōto no yatsu oshikko chibitta n' da.

The roller coaster was so fast that my little brother ended up peeing in his pants.

☞ Small children.

2. Be tight, stingy, tightfisted.

叔父さんはお金をちびって、ぼくにお小遣いもくれやしないよ。

Oji-san wa okane o chibitte, boku ni okozukai mo kure ya shinai yo.

My uncle's such a tightwad that he won't even give me any spending money.

chiyahoya suru (ちやほやする) "to coddle, pamper" Ⓥ Make a fuss (scene) over, stroke, flatter, sweet talk, soft-soap.

まわりの男の子にチヤホヤされて、彼女いい気になってるんだ。

Mawari no otoko no ko ni chiyahoya sarete, kanojo ii ki ni natte 'ru n' da.

She's really diggin' it the way all the guys make such a big deal over her.

chonbo (ちょんぼ) "a clinker" Ⓝ Ⓥ (suru) Fuck up, screw up, blow.

あいつのチョンボのせいで、ぼくたちの予定が狂っちゃったぜ。

Aitsu no chonbo no sei de, boku-tachi no yotei ga kurutchatta ze.

Our plans have been shot to pieces, thanks to him screwing up.

ゆるい一塁ゴロをチョンボして、うしろにそらしてしまったぜ。

Yurui ichirui-goro o chonbo shite, ushiro ni sorashite shimatta ze.

He blew an easy grounder to first, and then let the ball get behind him.

☞ Youth. From mah-jongg terminology.

choromakasu (ちょろまかす) "to pull a fast one" Ⅴ Swipe, requisition, steal, rip off.

あの人、店の売上金をちょろまかして競馬につぎ込んでいたの。

Ano hito, mise no uriage-kin o choromakashite keiba ni tsugikonde ita no.

That guy was dipping into (had his hand in) the till and playing the ponies.

☞ See also *pakuru*.

daberu (ダべる) "to make idle talk" Ⅴ Shoot the breeze, shoot the shit, chew the fat, bullshit, chinwag.

連中は、図書館でダべるだけで本なんか借りないんだ。

Renchū wa, tosho-kan de daberu dake de hon nanka karinai n' da.

All those guys do in the library is bullshit. They never check out any books.

☞ Student use. Verbalization of the now largely dead noun *daben* (駄弁; "foolish talk").

daburu (ダブる) "to duplicate" Ⅴ

1. Double up, be repetitive; [of televisions] have a ghost.

アンテナの受信具合が悪くて、うちのテレビは画面がダブるわ。

Antena no jushin-guai ga warukute, uchi no terebi wa gamen ga daburu wa.

Our TV antenna's all screwed up, so there's always a ghost on the screen.

2. [Student use] flunk, (have to) repeat.

必修科目の単位を落としちゃって、1年ダブることになったよ。

Hisshū-kamoku no tan'i o otoshichatte, ichinen daburu koto ni natta yo.

I've gotta repeat my freshman year 'cause I flunked a required class.

3. [Baseball] get two, get a double play.

練習試合はついてなくて、ファーストライナーでダブられたぜ。

Renshū-jiai wa tsuite 'nakute, fāsuto-rainā de daburareta ze.

I had some tough luck in one of our intrasquad games. Hit a liner to first right into a double play.

☞ Verbalized from English "double."

daihen suru (代返する) "to reply by proxy" Ⓥ Answer (the roll call) for someone.

あたし、これからデートなんで、悪いけど代返しといてくれない。

Atashi, kore kara dēto nan de, warui kedo daihen shitoite kurenai.

I've got a date, so would you mind answering for me when the roll's called?

☞ Student use.

datsusara (脱サラ) "to escape the salary(man's life)" Ⓝ Ⓥ *(suru)* Quit one's job as a businessman, get out of the rat race.

脱サラの人は、将来の人生設計を真剣に考えてる人が多いね。

Datsusara no hito wa, shōrai no jinsei-sekkei o shinken ni kangaete 'ru hito ga ōi ne.

Most people who drop out of the rat race have given a lot of thought to what they want to do with their lives.

☞ Abbreviation of *datsu-sararīman.*

dekiru (できる) "to be able to do, create, bear fruit" Ⓥ [Of an unmarried couple] have something going; be getting it on.

うちの主人は、ずいぶん前からあの女とできていたらしいのよ。

Uchi no shujin wa, zuibun mae kara ano onna to dekite ita rashii no yo.

I've got reason to believe that my husband's had something going with that woman for some time now.

deredere suru (でれでれする) "to be lax, slipshod" Ⓥ [Of a man] play up to (a woman), try to get in good with (a woman).

女性の前にでるとでれでれするような男には魅力を感じないわ。

Josei no mae ni deru to deredere suru yō na otoko ni wa miryoku o kanjinai wa.

Guys that fall all over themselves every time they meet a girl leave me cold.

detchi-ageru (でっちあげる) "to mix (up)" Ⓥ Trump up, make up, cook up.

サツはうその証拠をでっちあげるのがうまいから、注意しろよ。

Satsu wa uso no shōko o detchi-ageru no ga umai kara, chūi shiro yo.

The fuzz are pros at trumping up evidence. So watch yourself!

☞ Originally huckster's argot, *detchi* (捏ち) means to complicate matters.

donchan-sawagi suru (どんちゃん騒ぎする) "cause a commotion with cymbals and drums" Ⓥ Raise hell, raise a ruckus, raise the roof, party, party on down.

文化祭のあとは、どんちゃん騒ぎして、朝まで飲みまくろうよ。

Bunka-sai no ato wa, donchan-sawagi shite, asa made nomimakurō yo.

Hey man, whadya' say we party the rest of the night once the school festival's over.

☞ From the sound of drums and cymbals associated with an army setting off on a campaign or entering battle.

doron suru (どろんする) "to boom on a drum" Ⅴ Skip, skip out, skip town, disappear (into the woodwork).

あいつは集金したお金をもってドロンするつもりだな。

Aitsu wa shūkin shita okane o motte doron suru tsumori da na.

I bet he's planning on skipping town with the money he got from collecting bills.

☞ From the sound (*doron*) of drums beating to signal the appearance or disappearance of ghosts in a play. See also *tonzura suru, zurakaru.*

dotsubo ni hamaru (どつぼにはまる) "be stuck in a vase" Ⅴ Be the pits, be up the creek, be up shit creek.

セールスで無理やりに化粧品を買わされて、どつぼにはまってしまったわ。

Sērusu de muriyari ni keshō-hin o kawasarete, dotsubo ni hamatte shimatta wa.

What a bummer! Some door-to-door salesman talked me into buying a bunch of stupid cosmetics.

☞ Youth. Vulgar. From the expression *tsubo ni hamaru* (壷に嵌まる), which has approximately the same meaning but lacks the emphatic *do*.

dotsuku (どつく) "to jab" Ⅴ Let someone have it.

上司にまたくだらん文句を言われたら、今度は絶対どつくぜ。

Jōshi ni mata kudaran monku o iwaretara, kondo wa zettai dotsuku ze.

Next time the boss lays into me for something stupid, I'm gonna let him have it.

何、えらそうに言うてんねん。どつくで、ほんまに。[Kansai dialect]

Nani, erasō ni iu ten nen. Dotsuku de, honma ni.

You don't quit shootin' off your mouth, I'm gonna stuff it with a knuckle sandwich!

☞ Originally Kansai dialect. Formed from *tsuku* (to poke) and the emphatic *do*. See also *ippatsu kamasu.*

ē kakko suru (ええカッコする／ええ格好する) "to cut a figure" Ⅴ

1. [Kansai dialect] look good, put on the dog, dress to the teeth.

あんた、そんなええカッコしてどこ行くん？

Anta, sonna ē kakko shite doko iku n'?

Where're you goin' all dressed up like that?

2. Put on a show, to grandstand.

あいつフェミニストぶって、女の前ですぐええカッコする。

Aitsu feminisuto-butte, onna no mae de sugu ē kakko suru.

Guy acts the perfect gentleman whenever there's a woman around, but it's just a put-on.

enko suru (えんこする) "to squat" Ⅴ

1. [Somewhat dated baby talk] sit down.

さあ、いい子だから、ここにエンコして待ってましょうね。

Sā, ii ko da kara, koko ni enko shite matte 'mashō ne.

Be a good boy now and sit here and wait, okay?

2. Break down, give up the ghost.

先週買ったばかりのあの新車、走るとすぐエンコするのよ。

Senshū katta bakari no ano shinsha, hashiru to sugu enko suru no yo.

That new car I bought only last week breaks down every time I get it out on the road.

etchi suru (エッチする) "to do the H" Ⅴ Do it, do the wild thing, get it on.

山本君、会社帰りに彼女とデートして、毎晩エッチするんだと。

Yamamoto-kun, kaisha-gaeri ni kanojo to dēto shite, maiban etchi suru n' da to.

Yamamoto's getting it on with that gal every night on his way home from work? I don't believe it.

☞ Possibly from the "h" (pronounced *etchi*) of *hentai,* the romanization of 変態, "pervert." Euphemistic usage among students and the entertainment world. As a noun, it can also refer to a lecherous person.

fōkasu suru (フォーカスする) "to focus" Ⅴ Scoop, get the dirt on.

友達が、有名な作家とデートしてるのをフォーカスされたのよ。

Tomodachi ga, yūmei na sakka to dēto shite 'ru no o fōkasu sareta no yo.

A friend of mine got scooped by a paparazzo when she was out with some famous author.

☞ From the sensationalist pictorial weekly *Focus.* Circa 1981. Usually in the passive tense.

forō suru (フォローする) "to follow up" Ⅴ Back (someone) up, pitch in, lend a (helping) hand.

一生懸命提案したのに、上司は何もフォローしてくれないんだ。

Isshō-kenmei teian shita no ni, jōshi wa nani mo forō shite kurenai n' da.

I pushed the matter as hard as I could, but my boss never goes to bat for me (throws his weight behind my ideas).

☞ Youth. From the English "follow."

gata-ochi (がた落ち) **"to fall with a clatter"** Ⓝ Ⓥ (*suru*) Fall, crash, crash and burn, plunge, plummet, tumble.

社長との関係がバレちゃって、社内の彼女の評判はガタ落ちよ。

Shachō to no kankei ga barechatte, shanai no kanojo no hyōban wa gata-ochi yo.

When it got out that there was some hanky-panky goin' on between her and the president, her reputation in the office went straight into a tailspin.

戦争勃発のせいで、今年の海外旅行者数はガタ落ちするだろう。

Sensō-boppatsu no sei de, kotoshi no kaigai-ryokōsha–sū wa gata-ochi suru darō.

The number of people traveling abroad this year is going to plunge, what with the war and all.

☞ *Gata* is from *gatagata* (primarily a rattling sound; secondarily, things coming apart at the seams).

gata ga kuru (がたがくる) **"a clattering comes"** Ⓥ Fall apart, hit the skids, go kaput.

もう10年もこの車に乗ったんだから、ガタがくるのも当然だ。

Mō jū-nen mo kono kuruma ni notta n' da kara, gata ga kuru no mo tōzen da.

Ten years I've driven this car. I guess you've gotta expect things to start coming apart.

☞ See note to previous entry.

gattsuku (がっつく) **"to glom on to"** Ⓥ Lust for, crave; [of eating] inhale, scarf (down), stuff one's face, tear into, wolf down.

そんなにがっつくなよ。食べるものはたくさんあるんだからさ。

Sonna ni gattsuku na yo. Taberu mono wa takusan aru n' da kara sa.

Hey, don't make such a pig out of yourself. There's plenty (of food) for everybody.

☞ Contemptuous. Most likely a combination of *gatsu* ("avaricious," as in *gatsu-gatsu to taberu* (eat like a pig, wolf down) and *tsuku* (to adhere to).

gennari suru (げんなりする) **"to be tired of"** Ⓥ

1. Get (be) fed up with, just want to chuck it all, be up to here with.

何回企画書を提出しても毎回やり直しじゃ、げんなりするよね。

Nan-kai kikaku-sho o teishutsu shite mo maikai yarinaoshi ja, gen-nari suru yo ne.

Hey, anybody'd wanna throw in the towel if they'd written up a proposal over and over only to be told to do it again.

2. Be pooped, fagged out, on one's last legs, draggin' ass.

徹夜で仕事したら、ご飯も食べられないほどげんなりするわよ。

Tetsuya de shigoto shitara, gohan mo taberarenai hodo gennari suru wa yo.

Maybe if you'd been up working all night, you'd be so fagged out that you couldn't eat, either.

gochatsuku (ごちゃつく) "to be cluttered" Ⓥ Be (all) messed up, be in a mess.

今、父が書斎の本を整理中で、家の中がごちゃついてるんだ。

Ima, chichi ga shosai no hon o seiri-chū de, ie no naka ga gocha-tsuite 'ru n' da.

The whole house is in a mess because my dad's rearranging the books in his study.

☞ *Gocha* most likely comes from *gochagocha* (cluttered).

gorogoro suru (ごろごろする) "to roll around" Ⓥ

1. Be no end of, lousy with, crawling with.

そんなありふれた企画なら、世間にゴロゴロしてるんじゃないか。

Sonna arifureta kikaku nara, seken ni gorogoro shite 'ru n' ja nai ka.

There's more ideas like that around than you can shake a stick at. / Ideas like that are a dime a dozen, my friend.

2. Kick back, lie around, goof off, loaf around, putz around.

お父さんは、休みの日は一日中、家の中でゴロゴロしてるんだ。

Otōsan wa, yasumi no hi wa ichinichi-jū, ie no naka de gorogoro shite 'ru n' da.

Whenever he's got a day off, my dad just kicks back around the house.

gureru (ぐれる) "to be out of kilter" Ⓥ Go bad, start acting up, fall through the cracks.

親にも学校の先生にも反抗ばかりして、あの子もぐれる年頃ね。

Oya ni mo gakkō no sensei ni mo hankō bakari shite, ano ko mo gu-reru toshigoro ne.

I guess she's at that age, you know. Rebelling against her parents and her teachers at school.

☞ The word apparently traces its origins back to *gurihama*, a partial reversal of *hamaguri* (a clam), meaning that things were out of order or didn't make sense. *Gurihama* became *gurehama*, then simply *gure*, from which the present verb developed.

gyafun to iwaseru (ギャフンと言わせる) "to make someone

say ugh" V Really fix, do a number on, do in, fix one's wagon, shoot someone down in flames.

あの野郎、裁判に訴えてでも、必ずギャフンと言わせてやるぞ。

Ano yarō, saiban ni uttaete de mo, kanarazu gyafun to iwasete yaru zo.

I'm gonna fix that bastard even if I have to take him to court to do it.

hamoru (ハモる) V [Of voices, tastes and the like] go together (perfectly).

槙岡姉妹の歌声は、ハモると本当にうっとりする美しい声だわ。

Makioka shimai no utagoe wa, hamoru to hontō ni uttori suru utsukushii koe da wa.

The Makioka sisters sing such beautiful harmony together that it really sends me.

このソースは、バターとクリームが絶妙にハモっておいしいな。

Kono sōsu wa, batā to kurīmu ga zetsumyō ni hamotte oishii na.

What an exquisite taste! The butter and cream in this sauce go perfect together.

☞ Shortened and verbalized from English "harmony."

hashigo suru (はしごする) "to do the ladder" V Barhop, bar crawl, pub crawl; go to eat or drink something other than alcohol at several places in a row.

部長と飲みに行くと、必ず店をはしごするから困っちゃうんだ。

Buchō to nomi ni iku to, kanarazu mise o hashigo suru kara komatchau n' da.

I hate to go out for a drink with the head of the department because it always turns into a barhop.

☞ Shortened form of *hashigo-nomi* ("ladder drinking").

hayaben suru (早弁する) "to do a quick box (lunch)" V [Of a lunch brought with one] eat early.

うちのクラスじゃ、2時限目になると大半の生徒が早弁するよ。

Uchi no kurasu ja, nijigen-me ni naru to taihan no seito ga hayaben suru yo.

Almost everyone in my class is scarfing by the time second period rolls around.

☞ Verbalized portmanteau word from *haya* or "early" and *ben*, shortened from *bentō* or "box lunch." Student use.

hebaru (へばる) "to flop down" V Be beat, burned out, bushed, dead on one's feet, dog-tired, done in, tapped out.

朝食も昼食も食べずに仕事してたんじゃ、へばるのも無理ない。

Chōshoku mo chūshoku mo tabezu ni shigoto shite 'ta n' ja, hebaru no mo muri nai.

You've gotta expect to be draggin' ass, workin' without eatin' breakfast or lunch.

☞ Probably a shortened version of *hetabaru* (to slump into a sitting position from exhaustion). See also *bateru*.

hikkakeru (ひっかける) "to hang something up (on a hook), to bag, to net" Ⓥ

1. Take in, pull the wool over someone's eyes.

詐欺師が、うちの家内をひっかけてお金をまきあげたんですよ。

Sagi-shi ga, uchi no kanai o hikkakete okane o makiageta n' desu yo.

Some guy fed my old lady a line and conned her out of a bunch of money.

2. [Usually about men] pick up, score; hit on, make a pass at, put the make on, put the moves on, talk (chat) up.

街でギャルをひっかけたいなら、自分もカッコよくなくっちゃ。

Machi de gyaru o hikkaketai nara, jibun mo kakko yoku nakutcha.

Guy's gotta look sharp if he wants to pick up chicks.

☞ See also *nanpa suru.*

hishageru (ひしゃげる) "to flatten" Ⓥ Get squashed, squished, flattened.

あたしのケーキの箱がひしゃげるほど、満員電車で押されたの。

Atashi no kēki no hako ga hishageru hodo, man'in-densha de osareta no.

The train was so crowded that the box of cakes I was carrying got crushed.

hitoppashiri suru (ひとっ走りする) "to make one run" Ⓥ Run out for, run down to (the store for something).

ビールがないわ。彼に酒屋さんへひとっ走りするように言って。

Bīru ga nai wa. Kare ni sakaya-san e hitoppashiri suru yō ni itte.

We're out of beer. Can you get him to run down to the liquor store for me?

☞ Corruption of *hito-hashiri.*

hodohodo ni suru (ほどほどにする) "to set a limit to" Ⓥ Stop when one has had enough, know how far to go.

たまにウオッカを飲むのもいいけどさ、ほどほどにするんだよ。

Tama ni uokka o nomu no mo ii kedo sa, hodohodo ni suru n' da yo.

There's nothing wrong with having a little vodka every now and then, but you gotta know where to draw the line.

☞ *Hodohodo* (程々) means, in duplicate, "just the right amount."

hojikuru (ほじくる) **"to dig into a hole and stir up (its occupants)"** [V] Dig up, ferret out, pry into.

人の過去をそんなにほじくるのは、決して良いことじゃないよ。

Hito no kako o sonna ni hojikuru no wa, kesshite yoi koto ja nai yo.

Digging into someone's past like that is nothing to be proud of.

hottoku (ほっとく) **"to let be"** [V] Leave alone, don't touch, let alone.

しばらくひとりきりになりたいの。ほっといてくれないかしら。

Shibaraku hitorikiri ni naritai no. Hottoite kurenai kashira.

I don't feel like being around anybody for a while. Could I get you to just leave me alone?

☞ Corruption of *hōtte oku* (to throw aside and leave, leave as is, leave unfinished).

ichamon o tsukeru (いちゃもんをつける) **"to tack on a word of complaint"** [V] Create trouble on a false pretext; pick a fight.

あそこの店にヤクザがいちゃもんをつけて、金を脅しとった。

Asoko no mise ni yakuza ga ichamon o tsukete, kane o odoshitotta.

The yakuza shook down that place on some trivial pretext.

ikareru (いかれる) **"to be gone"** [V]

1. Go crazy, come unglued, crack up, go off one's nut, loose it.

あまり一生懸命勉強しすぎると、そのうち頭がいかれるぞ。

Amari isshō-kenmei benkyō shisugiru to, sono uchi atama ga ikareru zo.

Hit the books too hard and you'll end up goin' off the deep end.

2. Be head over heels in love with, gone on, crazy about, have the hots for.

一目見たときから、おれはありさちゃんにいかれちゃったよ。

Hitome mita toki kara, ore wa Arisa-chan ni ikarechatta yo.

I've had the hots for Arisa since I first laid eyes on her.

3. Be junk, run down, a piece of shit, on the blink, busted, ain't worth shit, have had it.

何度も落っことしたから、このウォークマンついにいかれたよ。

Nando mo okkotoshita kara, kono uōkuman tsui ni ikareta yo.

I've dropped this Walkman so many times that it finally gave up the ghost.

ikigaru (いきがる) **"to act stylish"** [V] Think that one is hot stuff, think (act like) one's shit doesn't stink.

たいして顔もスタイルもよくないのに、いきがるのはやめてよ。

Taishite kao mo sutairu mo yoku nai no ni, ikigaru no wa yamete yo.

With nothing going for you in the looks department and with taste like you've got, don't you think you ought'a stop actin' like you're God's gift to women?

☞ A verbalization (with the negatively nuanced *-garu*) of *iki* (粋; chic, smart, stylish).

ippai yaru (一杯やる) "to do one drink" Have a drink, tip one back, bend some elbows.

帰りに駅前の赤ちょうちんで一杯やりましょう。

Kaeri ni eki-mae no akachōchin de ippai yarimashō.

You got time for a drink on the way home at that little hole in the wall near the station?

☞ *Ippai* is a counter for drinks in glasses and cups. Often used by men when inviting someone out. *Aka-chōchin* (red lantern) is a reference to small drinking establishments that traditionally hung out a red lantern during business hours.

ippatsu kamasu (一発かます) "to have someone bite a bullet" Ⓥ Let someone have it, open up on someone.

口で言っても理解しないやつには、一発かましてわからせるか？

Kuchi de itte mo rikai shinai yatsu ni wa, ippatsu kamashite waka-raseru ka?

If we can't talk any sense into the mother, whad'ya say we lean on him a little?

☞ *Ippatsu* originally meant a shot from a bow or gun, or the bullet or arrow so shot. *Kamasu* (from 食わせる; *kuwaseru*, to force to eat) is colloquial for to say, do, or "let someone have it." See also *dotsuku*.

ippatsu-shōbu (一発勝負) "a one-shot match" Ⓝ A single game, match or bout on which everything is riding.

森さんは、親の遺産をそっくり賭博にかけて一発勝負したよ。

Mori-san wa, oya no isan o sokkuri tobaku ni kakete ippatsu-shōbu shita yo.

Mori gambled his entire inheritance on one roll of the die.

irekomu (いれこむ) "to pack in" Ⓥ Be hopped up about, be crazy about.

うちの社長は赤字覚悟で、文化事業にいれこむことに決めたの。

Uchi no shachō wa akaji kakugo de, bunka-jigyō ni irekomu koto ni kimeta no.

My boss made up his mind to throw the weight of the company behind cultural ventures even if it meant dipping into red ink.

その監督は、無名の新人女優にかなりいれこんでいるらしいよ。

Sono kantoku wa, mumei no shinjin-joyū ni kanari irekonde iru rashii yo.

Word is that the director is betting everything on some unknown actress.

jikoru (事故る) "to have an accident" Ⓥ Get in an accident, get in a fender-bender, cause an accident.

小林さんの運転なら事故るはずがないのに、昨日事故ったんだって。

Kobayashi-san no unten nara jikoru hazu ga nai no ni, kinō jikotta n' datte.

I never imagined that someone as good behind the wheel as Kobayashi would get in a fender-bender, but that's exactly what happened yesterday.

☞ Youth. A verbalization of the common noun *jiko* (accident).

jōhatsu suru (蒸発する) "to evaporate" Ⓥ Disappear, disappear into the woodwork, go underground.

君のお父さんが急に蒸発するなんて、いったい理由はなんだったんだろう。

Kimi no otōsan ga kyū ni jōhatsu suru nante, ittai riyū wa nan datta n' darō.

I wonder what ever caused your old man to just up and vanish like that?

☞ Since 1967.

jūden suru (充電する) "to recharge (a battery)" Ⓥ Kick back for a while, get some R and R.

彼みたいな流行作家には、時どき充電する期間が必要なんだよ。

Kare mitai na ryūkō sakka ni wa, tokidoki jūden suru kikan ga hitsu-yō nan da yo.

A popular writer like him has to take some time off now and then and get his creative juices flowing again.

kanningu (カンニング) Ⓝ Ⓥ (*suru*) Cheat, crib.

カンニングが見つかって、ぼくの数学の成績はFになったんだ。

Kanningu ga mitsukatte, boku no sūgaku no seiseki wa efu ni natta n' da.

I got an F in math 'cause I got caught cheating.

勉強不足だからって、試験場でカンニングするのは不可能だね。

Benkyō-busoku da kara tte, shiken-jō de kanningu suru no wa fukanō da ne.

I don't care if you haven't studied. No way you're gonna get away with cheating on the test.

☞ Student use. From the English "cunning."

kantetsu (完徹) Ⓝ Ⓥ (*suru*) Stay up all night, not sleep a wink, burn the midnight oil.

彼は毎晩残業していて、月に10日は完徹の日があるんだって。

Kare wa maiban zangyō shite ite, tsuki ni tōka wa kantetsu no hi ga aru n' datte.

He told me that he went without any sleep at all about ten days a month because of all the overtime he's got to put in. / He told me he works overtime every night, and at least ten days a month doesn't get a wink of sleep.

会議に間に合うように、山本さんは企画書を完徹して書いたんだ。

Kaigi ni ma ni au yō ni, Yamamoto-san wa kikaku-sho o kantetsu shi-te kaita n' da.

Yamamoto pulled an all-nighter on the proposal to have it ready for the meeting.

☞ Abbreviation of *kanzen-tetsuya* (完全徹夜; complete all-nighter).

kanzume ni naru/suru (かんづめになる／する) "to be/get canned" Ⓥ Get stuck (be locked up) somewhere; hole up (somewhere to get some work done).

今朝の停電で、鈴木は会社のエレベーターに4時間もかんづめになった。

Kesa no teiden de, Suzuki wa kaisha no erebētā ni yo-jikan mo kanzume ni natta.

Suzuki got stuck in the elevator at work for four hours this morning when the electricity went off.

あの作家はホテルにかんづめにすると良く書けるという評判だ。

Ano sakka wa hoteru ni kanzume ni suru to`yoku kakeru to iu hyōban da.

That author's famous for being able to write up a storm if you stick him (make him hole him up) in a hotel away from everything.

☞ *Kanzume* (缶詰) is "canned goods."

kapparau (かっぱらう) "to mow down" Ⓥ Snitch, steal, rip off.

代々木公園には、観光客からカメラをかっぱらう泥棒がいるらしい。

Yoyogi-kōen ni wa, kankō-kyaku kara kamera o kapparau dorobō ga iru rashii.

There's supposed to be some guy in Yoyogi Park who's ripping off tourists' cameras.

☞ The kanji are 掻っ払う.

kara-shutchō (空出張) "empty business trip" Ⓝ Ⓥ (*suru*) Pay (receive) travel expenses for an official (a business) trip not actually taken.

岩田は、空出張して会社のお金をごまかしていたのがバレた。

Iwata wa, kara-shutchō shite kaisha no okane o gomakashite ita no ga bareta.

Iwata got caught lining his own pockets with company funds by claiming travel expenses for trips he never took.
☞ Since 1979, when such practices among public officials began to make the news.

kīpu suru (キープする) V

1. Save, put away.

駅前のカラオケスナックにボトルをキープしてあるから行こう。

Eki-mae no karaoke-sunakku ni botoru o kīpu shite aru kara ikō.

I've got a bottle (They keep a bottle behind the bar for me) at that Karaoke bar near the station, so why don't we go there?

2. [Youth] string a guy (girl) along just in case things don't work out with one's main squeeze.

まず彼女を恋人にキープして、そのあとで本命にアタックする。

Mazu kanojo o koibito ni kīpu shite, sono ato de honmei ni atakku suru.

Once I've got her in my pocket I'll hit on the one I really like. / I'm gonna land this one first, then I'll see what I can do to reel in the big one.
☞ From the English "keep."

kiseru (キセル) "a smoking pipe" N V (*suru*) Ride (riding) the train free for part of a journey or commute by buying only the tickets necessary to get on the train and get off it.

キセルで乗車区間をごまかすことは、りっぱな詐欺罪になるわ。

Kiseru de jōsha-kukan o gomakasu koto wa, rippa na sagi-zai ni naru wa.

Riding the trains without buying a ticket for the whole trip is fraud, pure and simple.

京都から東京までキセルして、東京駅では定期券で駅をでたよ。

Kyōto kara Tōkyō made kiseru shite, Tōkyō-eki de wa teiki-ken de eki o deta yo.

I rode all the way from Kyoto to Tokyo by just showing my pass when I left Tokyo Station.
☞ From a now-defunct narrow, long-stemmed pipe by the same name which has a metal bowl and mouthpiece, but a stem of some other material. The word *kiseru* itself comes from the Cambodian "khsier," meaning "tube" or "pipe."

kokiorosu (こきおろす) "to strip down" V Bad mouth, jack up, jump all over, knock, put down, run down, trash.

評論家は、あの映画をこきおろしていた。

Hyōron-ka wa, ano eiga o kokioroshite ita.

The critics were really panning that movie.
☞ *Kokiorosu* (扱き下ろす) seems to have originally meant "strip down or off"—that is, to remove the leaves from the stock of a plant. *Koku* = strip, thresh.

kokitsukau (こき使う) "to strip down and use" V Be a slave driver, drive (work) someone hard.

うちの会社は、人をこき使うようなひどい会社なのよ。

Uchi no kaisha wa, hito o kokitsukau yō na hidoi kaisha na no yo.

They work you like it was the salt mines at my office. It's simply awful.

☞ See note to previous entry.

koku (こく) "to excrete (from the body)" V

1. [Vulgar] fart, let a fart, cut the cheese, lay one, rip one off.

おれの部屋で屁をこくな。おまえの屁はほんとに臭いんだから。

Ore no heya de he o koku na. Omae no he wa honto ni kusai n' da kara.

Don't be cuttin' farts in my room. They stink to high heaven.

2. [Vulgar] say, go, blow off one's trap, shoot off one's mouth.

あいつはうそばかりこくから、絶対に信用しちゃいけないんだ。

Aitsu wa uso bakari koku kara, zettai ni shin'yō shicha ikenai n' da.

Don't believe a word he says. He lies through his teeth all the time.

kubippiki (首っ引き) "neck-pulling" N Constant reference to something.

辞書と首っ引きでなきゃ、ぼくにはチョーサーは読めないな。

Jisho to kubippiki de nakya, boku ni wa Chōsā wa yomenai na.

There's no way I can read Chaucer without having my nose in a dictionary all the time.

☞ From *kubihiki* (same kanji), a kind of tug of war in which two people put their heads through a loop and pulled against one another.

kutabaru (くたばる) "to languish" V Drop dead, kick the bucket, croak, buy it, check out.

もうあのじじいもくたばるさ。そうすりゃ、あんたも楽になる。

Mō ano jijī mo kutabaru sa. Sō surya, anta mo raku ni naru.

The old bugger'll croak pretty soon and things'll start lookin' up for ya.

☞ See also *hebaru*.

kuttsukeru (くっつける) "to stick together" V Fix two people up; marry someone off.

仲間で、太郎さんと花子さんをくっつけるお膳立てをやろうよ。

Nakama de, Tarō-san to Hanako-san o kuttsukeru ozen-date o yarō yo.

Hey, man, let's all see if we can fix Taro and Hanako up with each other.

kuu (食う) "to hold in the mouth" Ⅴ

1. [Male usage] eat, feed one's face, scarf, chow down.

おい、おれの家に寄って、帰りにメシでも食っていかないかい？

Oi, ore no ie ni yotte, kaeri ni meshi de mo kutte ikanai kai?

Hey, man, you wanna stop by my place on the way home and put the feed bag on?

2. Bite, feed on.

田舎に行ったら、やたらと蚊と蚤に食われてまいっちゃったよ。

Inaka ni ittara, yatara to ka to nomi ni kuwarete maitchatta yo.

I got eaten alive by fleas and mosquitos when I went out into the country. It was a real bummer.

3. Whip (someone stronger than oneself), do a number on someone; horn in on one's territory.

前座で歌った新人の歌手が、人気演歌歌手を食ってしまったね。

Zenza de utatta shinjin no kashu ga, ninki–enka-kashu o kutte shi-matta ne.

The new singer that appeared at the beginning of the program sure stole the thunder from that popular enka singer, didn't she?

4. Suffer something, get something undesirable.

もしそんなに帰りが遅くなったら、お父さんに大目玉を食うわ。

Moshi sonna ni kaeri ga osoku nattara, otōsan ni ōmedama o kuu wa.

God, if I came home that late my dad would really lay into me.

5. Waste, end up spending.

成田空港まで交通渋滞にぶつかって１時間もよけいに食ったぜ。

Narita-kūkō made kōtsū-jūtai ni butsukatte ichi-jikan mo yokei ni kutta ze.

I lost an hour in a traffic jam on the way to Narita.

maku (まく) "to roll up" Ⅴ Lose, ditch.

さっきからずっと刑事が尾行してるみたいだ。うまくまくんだ。

Sakki kara zutto keiji ga bikō shite 'ru mitai da. Umaku maku n' da.

Looks like some dick's been tailing us for a while. Let's ditch him.

marumekomu (まるめこむ) "to roll up and put inside" Ⅴ Sell someone on something, talk someone into doing something, take someone in; have someone in one's pocket, have someone wrapped around one's little finger.

あいつ、自分の弟をまるめこんで悪いことを企んでるらしい。

Aitsu, jibun no otōto o marumekonde warui koto o takurande 'ru ra-shii.

By the looks of things, he's draggin' his little brother into some caper he's planning.

me ga ten ni naru (目が点になる) "the eyes become specks" Ⓥ
Be floored, be bug-eyed, be blown away.

彼のダサイ格好を見たら、あんただって目が点になるはずよ。

Kare no dasai kakkō o mitara, anta datte me ga ten ni naru hazu yo.

You'd have been blown away too if you'd seen the stupid way he was dressed.

☞ Used among young people. From the practice of cartoonists using dots to represent the eyes of characters who are surprised.

miyako-ochi suru (都落ちする) "to drop from the capital" Ⓥ
Be (demoted and) transferred out of a central metropolitan area into the country; leave the big city to work in the country.

この計画で失敗したら、いなかの支社に都落ちするしかないね。

Kono keikaku de shippai shitara, inaka no shisha ni miyako-ochi suru shika nai ne.

If this project flops, I'll end up in some branch office out in the sticks.

naishoku suru (内職する) "to do inside work" Ⓥ Do homework for one class during another; eat lunch during class; work on something during a meeting.

先生の講義も聞かずに、内職して次の時間の予習をすませたわ。

Sensei no kōgi mo kikazu ni, naishoku shite tsugi no jikan no yoshū o sumaseta wa.

I didn't pay any attention to what the prof was saying. Just got ready for my next class.

☞ From duties in the inner sanctum of a palace, *naishoku* took on the meaning of work other than one's main occupation: i.e., "moonlighting" or a second job or sideline, from which the present meaning developed.

nameru (なめる) "to lick (with the tongue)" Ⓥ Treat someone bad, treat someone like shit; take someone for a fool, don't take someone (or something) seriously.

あんた、あたしが年下の女だからってさ、なめるんじゃないよ！

Anta, atashi ga toshishita no onna da kara tte sa, nameru n' ja nai yo!

What do you take me for, treating me like that just because I'm a woman and younger than you?

nanpa suru (軟派する) "to do the soft faction" Ⓥ Pick up.

金も車もなしで、渋谷に行って女をナンパするのは不可能だよ。

Kane mo kuruma mo nashi de, Shibuya ni itte onna o nanpa suru no wa fu-kanō da yo.

No way you're gonna be able to pick up a chick in Shibuya without a
car or money.

☞ Derived originally from "a faction without a strong opinion" and the derivative
"(school of) entertainers who favor the use of eroticism." See also *hikkakeru*.

neko-kawaigari (猫かわいがり) "to be affectionate to one's cat"
Ⓝ Ⓥ (*suru*) Dote on.

猫かわいがりなしつけ方法は、わがままな子供を育てるだけだ。

*Neko-kawaigari na shitsuke-hōhō wa, wagamama na kodomo o
sodateru dake da.*

If you're too easy on your kids, they'll end up being self-centered.

ocha suru (お茶する) "to have some tea" Ⓥ
1. Go to a coffee shop; have a cup of coffee.

明日の午後、北山通りのおしゃれなカフェでお茶するのよ。

*Ashita no gogo, Kitayama-dōri no oshare na kafe de ocha suru no
yo.*

Tomorrow afternoon we're going to a chic coffee shop on Kitayama
Avenue, I'll have you know.
2. [A pick-up line] have a cup of coffee.

ねえ彼女、ちょっとそこらでお茶しない？おれがおごるからさ。

Nē kanojo, chotto sokora de ocha shinai? Ore ga ogoru kara sa.

Hey baby, how 'bout having a cup of coffee with me? My treat.
☞ Youth.

ochokuru (おちょくる) "to touch playfully" Ⓥ Tease, make fun
of, make a fool of, razz, slam.

子供のくせにおれの面倒を見てやるだと。大人をおちょくるな。

*Kodomo no kuse ni ore no mendō o mite yaru da to. Otona o ocho-
kuru na.*

Kid like you talking about how you'll look after me! You shouldn't
make fun of your elders like that. (Let's have a little more respect
for your elders.)
☞ Characteristically Kansai usage.

odabutsu (お陀仏) Ⓝ Ⓥ (*suru*)
1. Die, kick the bucket, go home feet first.

飛行機はとても便利だけど、一度墜落したら全員おダブツだよな。

*Hikō-ki wa totemo benri da kedo, ichido tsuiraku shitara zen'in
odabutsu da yo na.*

Planes are great for getting around, but once there's a crash, then
that's all she wrote.
2. Go up in smoke, (go) belly up, go bust, fold.

あてにしていた助成金がもらえなくて、この計画はお陀仏だよ。

Ate ni shite ita josei-kin ga moraenakute, kono keikaku wa odabutsu da yo.

The grant I was counting on didn't come through, so we can kiss this project good-bye.

☞ From the last three syllables of the Buddhist chant *Namu amida-butsu* ("Praise the great Amitabha"), recited upon a person's death in the belief that the deceased will thereby be transported to the Pure Land.

onbu suru (おんぶする) "to carry on the back" Ⓥ

1. Carry someone (especially a child) piggyback.

パパ、おんぶしてちょうだい。あたし、疲れちゃったんだもん。

Papa, onbu shite chōdai. Atashi, tsukarechatta n' da mon.

Daddy, give me a piggyback ride, please. I'm all tired out.

2. Bum off, sponge on, leach on, mooch off.

あいつは、自分の生活費を全額両親におんぶすることにしてる。

Aitsu wa, jibun no seikatsu-hi o zengaku ryōshin ni onbu suru koto ni shite 'ru.

He's sponging on his parents for all his living expenses.

orei-mairi (お礼参り) "to offer thanks" Ⓝ Ⓥ (suru) Settle an old score, seek revenge (after one gets out of prison or graduates from school) for things done to one.

ヤクザのお礼参りが恐ろしくて誰も裁判で証言してくれないらしい。

Yakuza no orei-mairi ga osoroshikute dare mo saiban de shōgen shite kurenai rashii.

Everybody's so afraid of getting a little visit from the yakuza that it looks like no one is going to testify.

兄貴は卒業式の日に先公たちへお礼参りするつもりらしい。

Aniki wa sotsugyō-shiki no hi ni senkō-tachi e orei-mairi suru tsumori rashii.

It sure looks like my big brother's going to return some favors to his teachers on graduation day.

☞ From the practice by the same name of visiting a temple or shrine to offer thanks to the gods or buddhas for a wish fulfilled.

pakuru (ぱくる) "to gulp (food)" Ⓥ

1. Steal, rip off, heist, lift, requisition.

他社のアイディアをぱくって、うちで商品化するなんて卑怯だよ。

Tasha no aidia o pakutte, uchi de shōhin-ka suru nante hikyō da yo.

It's really underhanded to rip off ideas from other companies and turn them into our own products.

2. Arrest, bust, collar, pick up, pinch, run in.

売人のほうはぱくられたが見張り役のやつが逃げちゃった。

Bainin no hō wa pakurareta ga mihari-yaku no yatsu ga nigechatta.

The dealer got nabbed, but his lookout got away.

☞ See also *choromakasu.*

pinhane suru (ピンはねする) "to flick off a tenth" Ⅴ Skim, siphon off (money), take a cut (off the top), rake off, pocket.

稼いだ金をヤクザがピンハネするから、ホステスの真知子はいつでも貧乏だ。

Kaseida kane o yakuza ga pinhane suru kara, hosutesu no Machiko wa itsu de mo binbō da.

The yakuza rake off part of what Machiko makes as a hostess, so she has a hell of a time making ends meet.

☞ Portmanteau word from *pin* of the Portuguese *pinta*, meaning "first," hence "one-tenth," and *hane* from *haneru* (撥ねる), meaning "to send flying" or, here, to take part of someone else's cut.

riki o ireru (リキを入れる) "put oomph into" Ⅴ Get into, work out.

大学3年の夏から、みんな就職活動にリキを入れるようになるんだ。

Daigaku sannen no natsu kara, minna shūshoku-katsudō ni riki o ireru yō ni naru n' da.

Everybody really gets into looking for a job when the summer of their junior year rolls around.

☞ Youth. *Riki* is a variant reading of *ryoku* (力).

ryōri suru (料理する) "to cook" Ⅴ

1. Handle, take care of, dispatch.

百貨店の顧客担当者は、お客の苦情をうまく料理して納得させた。

Hyakka-ten no kokyaku–tantō-sha wa, okyaku no kujō o umaku ryōri shite nattoku saseta.

The customer complaint desk of the department store made short work of that complaint and completely satisfied the customer.

2. Fix, do a job on; kill, rub out, snuff, waste, blow away.

もう二度と口がきけないように、おまえをじっくり料理するぜ。

Mō nido to kuchi ga kikenai yō ni, omae o jikkuri ryōri suru ze.

We're gonna cook your goose so you'll never go shootin' off your mouth again.

saboru (サボる) Ⅴ Goldbrick, ditch (school), cut (class); call in sick (at work).

山田さんはこのごろ、風邪をひいたとうそついて会社をさぼるのよ。

Yamada-san wa konogoro, kaze o hiita to uso tsuite kaisha o saboru no yo.

Yamada's been calling in sick these days, letting on that he's down with a cold.

☞ Shortened, verbalized form of the French "sabotage."

shasharideru (しゃしゃり出る) "to come out willy-nilly" Ⓥ
Horn in, butt in, poke one's nose in (someone else's business).

オバタリアンはなんにでもしゃしゃり出るから、嫌われるのよ。

Obatarian wa nan ni de mo shasharideru kara, kirawareru no yo.

Pushy old women are always sticking their noses in where they don't belong. That's why they've got such a bad reputation.

shigoku (しごく) "to strip" Ⓥ Haze, teach someone a lesson, drive someone hard.

テニス部の新入部員を、こってりしごくのが先輩の役目なのさ。

Tenisu-bu no shinnyū-buin o, kotteri shigoku no ga senpai no yaku-me na no sa.

Putting the new guys on the tennis team through the wringer, that's the job of the upperclassmen.

なんや、おまえ生意気やな。ちょっとしごいたろか。(Kansai dialect)

Nan ya, omae namaiki ya na. Chotto shigoitaro ka.

Whoa, got a real smart ass here. See I'm gonna hav'ta teach you a lesson.

☞ Originally "to strip (leaves from a plant)."

shikato suru (しかとする) "to do a ten-point deer" Ⓥ Give someone the cold shoulder, leave someone out, don't give someone the time of day.

クラスの仲間にしかとされ、ぼくだけコンパに誘われなかった。

Kurasu no nakama ni shikato sare, boku dake konpa ni sasoware-nakatta.

The whole class gave me the cold shoulder. I was the only one who didn't get invited to the party.

☞ The deer on the ten-point card "fall colors and deer" in the Japanese card game *hanafuda* is facing left with its body, but looking behind and to the right with its head (as if ignoring something). Hence, "the ten-point deer" (鹿十; *shikatō*) became *shikato*. Originally gamblers' argot.

shippo o dasu (しっぽを出す) "to show one's tail" Ⓥ Show one's true colors, slip up (and be found out).

あんたがどんなに頭がいいドロボウだって、いつかはしっぽを出して捕まってしまうんだわ。

Anta ga donna ni atama ga ii dorobō datte, itsu ka wa shippo o da-shite tsukamatte shimau n' da wa.

I don't care how clever a burglar you are, eventually you'll slip up and get caught.

☞ From the belief that some animals, such as the fox, which can assume human form, eventually reveal their true identity by inadvertently exposing their tails.

shirinugui (尻拭い) "butt wiping" Ⓝ Ⓥ (suru) Clean up after someone, straighten out someone's mess.

君の借金の尻拭いまで、なぜぼくがしなければならないんだ。

Kimi no shakkin no shirinugui made, naze boku ga shinakereba naranai n' da.

Why the hell do I have to take care of everything for you, debts and all?

いまどき、部下の不始末を尻拭いする上司なんていやしないよ。

Imadoki, buka no fu-shimatsu o shirinugui suru jōshi nante iya shinai yo.

You're not going to find many bosses nowadays who'll cover for the people under them when they screw up.

☞ Originally, to wipe oneself after a bowel movement. *Nugui* is from the verb *nuguu* (to wipe).

shō-ene (省エネ) "curtail energy" Ⓝ Energy (resource) conservation. Ⓥ (suru) Save energy, conserve energy.

君もこまめに電気のスイッチを消して、省エネに協力しなさい。

Kimi mo komame ni denki no suitchi o keshite, shō-ene ni kyōryoku shinasai.

Get with the program here and help save energy by turning off the lights whenever you're not using them.

省エネするつもりなら、まず朝のシャワーをやめたらどうだい？

Shō-ene suru tsumori nara, mazu asa no shawā o yametara dō dai?

If you're serious about conserving resources, why not give up your morning shower?

☞ Shortened from *shō-enerugī*. Since 1979.

suberu (すべる) "to slip (lose one's footing)" Ⓥ Not pass an admission test to school, not be admitted to school.

あんたが東大をすべるのは当然だよ。浪人して勉強しなさいよ。

Anta ga Tōdai o suberu no wa tōzen da yo. Rōnin shite benkyō shinasai yo.

You didn't really expect to get into Tokyo University, did you? Give it another shot after you hit the books for a year.

suppanuku (すっぱぬく) "to unsheathe unexpectedly" Ⓥ Expose, reveal, disclose, blow.

芸能記者が、政治家と映画女優のスキャンダルをすっぱぬいた。

Geinō-kisha ga, seiji-ka to eiga-joyū no sukyandaru o suppanuita.

Some paparazzo blew the lid off a scandal involving a politician and a movie star.

☞ Originally, to draw one's sword without warning. *Nuku* is "draw," and *suppa* apparently refers back to the scout who was selected from among local bandits and other dubious armed characters to lead the troops of a warring daimyo through unfamiliar territory.

suppokasu (すっぽかす) "to dump" Ⅴ

1. Shirk, neglect, shine.

ぼくの弟は宿題をすっぽかして、どっかに遊びに行っちゃった。

Boku no otōto wa shukudai o suppokashite, dokka ni asobi ni itchatta.

My little brother shined (skipped, pigeonholed) his homework and went outside to play.

2. Stand up, break an engagement.

あの男は、人の約束をすっぽかすので有名なの。

Ano otoko wa, hito no yakusoku o suppokasu no de yūmei na no.

He's positively notorious for standing up his dates.

☞ Emphatic form of *hokasu* (discard, leave as is). *Su* indicates an extreme condition.

tobasareru (とばされる) "to be sent flying" Ⅴ Be sent down, be

posted in the sticks somewhere.

この計画に失敗したら、君は本社から地方にとばされるだろう。

Kono keikaku ni shippai shitara, kimi wa honsha kara chihō ni tobasareru darō.

You're going to be out in some branch office in the middle of nowhere if this project of yours flops.

tonbogaeri (トンボ帰り) "a dragonfly's return" Ⓝ Ⅴ (*suru*) Go

somewhere to take care of business and come right back without staying the night.

朝一番で東京から大阪へ行き、トンボ帰りで東京に戻るんだ。

Asa ichiban de Tōkyō kara Ōsaka e iki, tonbogaeri de Tōkyō ni modoru n' da.

I'm leaving Tokyo first thing in the morning for Osaka and then coming right back.

パリ・ロンドン間をトンボ帰りする出張なんて、無謀すぎるよ。

Pari-Rondon–kan o tonbogaeri suru shutchō nante, mubō sugiru yo.

Going back and forth on business between Paris and London in the same day is just too much (ridiculous).

☞ From the quick directional changes of dragonflies (*tonbo*) in flight.

tonzura suru (とんずらする) "(to do an) amscray" Ⅴ Skip out,

beat feet, split, get away, hightail it, make a getaway.

あの野郎、分け前だけ取ったらとんずらするつもりに違いない。

Ano yarō, wakemae dake tottara tonzura suru tsumori ni chigai-nai.

Asshole's gonna take his cut and split. I can see it now.

☞ Formerly criminal argot. Portmanteau word from *ton* of *tonsō* (遁走), which means flight or escape, and *zura* of the verb *zurakaru*, slang for "get away or beat feet." See also *doron suru*, *zurakaru*.

totchimeru (とっちめる) "to take control of" Ⓥ Grill, bear down on, give someone the third degree; beat the shit out of, lay into, teach someone a lesson.

知事の不祥事を会議で公にして、やつをとっちめるのが一番だ。

Chiji no fu-shōji o kaigi de ōyake ni shite, yatsu o totchmeru no ga ichiban da.

I say, let's hang the governor's dirty laundry out at the meeting and rake him over the coals.

☞ A corruption of *torishimeru* (control, regulate).

tsumamigui suru (つまみ食いする) "to pick up (with one's fingers) and eat" Ⓥ

1. Dip into, siphon off.

市役所の会計課長は、密かに公金をつまみ食いしていたらしい。

Shi-yakusho no kaikei-kachō wa, hisoka ni kōkin o tsumamigui shite ita rashii.

The head of the accounting section at city hall seems to have been pocketing small amounts of public money.

2. Play the field, play around; lay (a woman without intending to stay with her for long), have a one-night stand.

映画監督は、新人女優をつまみ食いするから気をつけなさいね。

Eiga-kantoku wa, shinjin-joyū o tsumamigui suru kara ki o tsuke-nasai ne.

Better watch yourself. Movie directors are always bedding young actresses like you.

tsumeru (つめる) "to stuff (pack) in" Ⓥ To look at (a plan etc.) more closely, fine-tune, get down to the nitty-gritty (the fine print).

新しい販売計画を実行に移す前に、もう一度手順をつめることが大切だな。

Atarashii hanbai-keikaku o jikkō ni utsusu mae ni, mō ichido tejun o tsumeru koto ga taisetsu da na.

It's best to work out the wrinkles in the new sales promotion plan before giving it the green light.

tsurumu (つるむ) "to take along" Ⓥ Hang out with someone.

あいつら、いつもつるんで恐喝をしたり万引きしたりしてるぜ。

Aitsu-ra, itsumo tsurunde kyōkatsu o shitari manbiki shitari shite 'ru ze.

Those dudes are always hanging out together, intimidating (strong-arming, bullying) people and shoplifting stuff.

☞ Youth. Originally criminal argot. While there is no clear etymological relationship other than that of pronunciation, it is intriguing to note that *tsurumu* (with different kanji) can also refer to copulation between animals.

yoisho suru (よいしょする) "to give a boost up" Ⓥ Butter up, soft-soap, brownnose, stroke, apple-polish.

秘書課の社員は社長をヨイショして、おだててばかりいるんだ。

Hisho-ka no shain wa shachō o yoisho shite, odatete bakari iru n' da.

Everyone in the secretarial section is always sucking up to the president.

☞ From the utterance *yoisho* (upsy-daisy, ally-oop), used when lifting heavy objects.

yoromeku (よろめく) "to stagger, be thrown off balance" Ⓥ [Of a married woman] to be seduced, have an affair, have a fling; two-time (one's husband).

若い男によろめく人妻を描いたメロドラマが、主婦に人気があるよ。

Wakai otoko ni yoromeku hitozuma o egaita merodorama ga, shufu ni ninki ga aru yo.

Soap operas about married women having affairs with younger men are really popular among housewives.

☞ From Yukio Mishima's 1957 novel *Bitoku no Yoromeki.*

zukkokeru (ずっこける) "to fall flat" Ⓥ

1. Fall down, trip.

400メートル走のゴール直前でずっこけるなんて君は最低だ。

Yonhyaku-mētoru-sō no gōru chokuzen de zukkokeru nante kimi wa saitei da.

What a dipshit! Falling flat on your face right in front of the finish line of the 400.

2. Slide off, fall off.

居眠りして椅子からずっこけて、クラスの人に笑われちゃった。

Inemuri shite isu kara zukkokete, kurasu no hito ni warawarechatta.

The whole class got a big laugh when I dozed off and fell off my chair.

3. Be a clown, clown around, be a joker, be a cutup, be the life of the party.

ポールはいつも人を笑わせて、ずっこけたおかしなやつなんだ。

Pōru wa itsumo hito o warawasete, zukkoketa okashi na yatsu nan da.

Paul's a real riot. He's always doing something to make people laugh.

4. Be a bummer, be a downer, be a letdown.

彼女にキスする瞬間に、もしおならしたら、ずっこけるだろうね。

Kanojo ni kisu suru shunkan ni, moshi onara shitara, zukkokeru darō ne.

What a drag it'd be if you let one right when you were kissing her.

☞ Emphatic form of *kokeru* (to fall, take a header).

zurakaru (ずらかる) "to do a powder" Ⓥ Split, beat feet, get out; go underground, hide, disappear (into the woodwork).

会社の金の横領に成功したら、すぐ外国にずらかるのが得策だ。

Kaisha no kane no ōryō ni seikō shitara, sugu gaikoku ni zurakaru no ga tokusaku da.

You'd be smart to split to some foreign country once you've succeeded in embezzling company money.

☞ Formerly criminal argot. See also *doron suru*, *tonzura suru*.

The Mind and Emotions:
Blazing, Quaking, and Serene Shenanigans

akkerakan (あっけらかん) "jolted" Ⓐ
1. Be stupefied, in (a state of) shock, flabbergasted, floored.

街を裸で歩いている男を、みんなあっけらかんと見ていた。

Machi o hadaka de aruite iru otoko o, minna akkerakan to mite ita.

Everyone just stood there with their mouths open, watching some guy walking naked through town.

2. Be cool, nonchalant, have a couldn't-care-less attitude.

あいつはへまをやらかしてもあっけらかんとしているんだよ。

Aitsu wa hema o yarakashite mo akkerakan to shite iru n' da yo.

He couldn't care less if he makes a mess of things. / It's all the same to him if he screws up or not.

☞ Also *akerakan*. Associated both by meaning and pronunciation with the standard *akke-nai* (呆気ない; disappointing) and *akke ni torareru* (呆気にとられる; to be jolted, startled).

betabore (ベタ惚れ) "to be flat-out amazed" Ⓥ Be head over heels in love with, really gone on, crazy about, carry the torch for.

あいつはなんにも言わないけど、本当は彼女にベタ惚れなのさ。

Aitsu wa nanni mo iwanai kedo, hontō wa kanojo ni betabore na no sa.

He doesn't talk about it, but he's really got this thing for her.

☞ From *beta*, meaning to completely cover a surface or to be adhering fast to a surface, and *bore*, a corruption of the verb *horeru*, the primary meaning of which is "to be dazed or bemused" but now also means to fall madly in love with.

bibiru (びびる) "to shrivel up" Ⓥ Lose one's nerve, be a 'fraidy (scaredy) cat, scared stiff.

急にヤクザにからまれたら、だれだってびびるに決まってるよ。

Kyū ni yakuza ni karamaretara, dare datte bibiru ni kimatte 'ru yo.

Anybody's asshole'd be suckin' wind if a bunch of yakuza started hassling him all of a sudden.

☞ Youth.

bikubiku suru (びくびくする) "to quake" Ⓥ Have a heart attack, be shaking in one's boots.

リッツに泊まるからってびくびくするなよ。金は払うんだから。

Rittsu ni tomaru kara tte bikubiku suru na yo. Kane wa harau n' da kara.

There is no reason to get all worked up just because we're staying at the Ritz. We're paying good, hard cash.

gingin (ぎんぎん) **"squeaking and squawking"** Ⓐ Rockin', be into it, one's hair is down.

おとなしいあの子も、AC/DCのコンサートではギンギンになる。

Otonashii ano ko mo, eishī-dīshī no konsāto de wa gingin ni naru.

She's usually pretty quiet, but you should'a seen her rockin' out at the AC/DC concert.

☞ Youth. Used initially about rock music itself. Originally from the raucous noise of chirping insects, it is perhaps not entirely irrelevant to mention that *gingin* can also refer to the pain of a splitting headache.

gutto kuru (ぐっとくる) **"to come welling up"** Ⓥ Really hit one, really get one, hit home.

彼のやさしいことばは、胸にぐっとくるわ。あたし、涙出そうよ。

Kare no yasashii kotoba wa, mune ni gutto kuru wa. Atashi, namida desō yo.

He says so many sweet things, it gets me right here. I could just cry.

hetchara (へっちゃら) **"serene shenanigans"** Ⓐ Nothing to get worked up about, no big deal, no great shakes, no sweat.

このくらいの傷なら、ほっておいてもへっちゃらさ。すぐ治るよ。

Kono kurai no kizu nara, hotte oite mo hetchara sa. Sugu naoru yo.

A little ding like that's no big deal. It'll take care of itself.

うちの子なんか怒られてもへっちゃらで、涙も流さないのよ。

Uchi no ko nanka okorarete mo hetchara de, namida mo nagasanai no yo.

A little scolding doesn't faze my daughter, much less make her cry.

☞ A corruption of *heichara*, which is a combination of the *hei* from *heiki* (平気, "serene spirit"; i.e., no problem) and *chara* (nonsense, trickery, shenanigans).

hisu (ヒス) Ⓝ Hysteria, hysterics.

ぼくの上司は女性で、人が変わったようにヒスをおこすんだ。

Boku no jōshi wa josei de, hito ga kawatta yō ni hisu o okosu n' da.

This woman I work for really comes unglued (goes into hysterics) sometimes.

☞ Shortened from the German "Hysterie."

hiyahiya (ヒヤヒヤ) **"chilly"** Ⓐⅾ Be beside oneself with fear, break out in a cold sweat, be waiting for the ax to fall.

母親の財布から１万円札を抜いたのがバレそうでヒヤヒヤなんだ。

Haha-oya no saifu kara ichiman'en-satsu o nuita no ga baresō de hiyahiya nan da.

I'm about to piss my pants 'cause it looks like my mom found out I swiped 10,000 yen out'a her purse.

kachin to kuru (カチンとくる) "to come with a clank" V Really get one, really piss one off, hit one right where it hurts.

あいつの生意気な態度には、上司のオレはいつもカチンとくる。

Aitsu no namaiki na taido ni wa, jōshi no ore wa itsumo kachin to kuru.

His smart-aleck attitude toward me—I'm his boss, for God's sake— really ticks me off.

kakka suru (カッカする) "to blaze" V Get one's balls in an uproar, get all hot and bothered, get all worked up.

僕の上司は、自分の指示に部下が反論するとすぐカッカする。

Boku no jōshi wa, jibun no shiji ni buka ga hanron suru to sugu kakka suru.

My boss flies off the handle every time one of us questions his orders.

kankan (かんかん) "clang" N Blow one's top, blow up, explode, throw a fit, lose it, lose one's cool.

大事にしていた壺を弟が割ったので、お父さんはかんかんなの。

Daiji ni shite ita tsubo o otōto ga watta no de, otōsan wa kankan na no.

My dad's really p.o.'d (bent out of shape) 'cause my little brother broke one of his favorite pots.

☞ Along with "clang," *kankan* has the primary meaning of "glaring" sunlight.

karikari suru (カリカリする) "to crunch (with the teeth)" V Be uptight, wound-up; to get edgy, antsy.

入試を目前にした姉貴は、勉強がはかどらずカリカリしてる。

Nyūshi o mokuzen ni shita aneki wa, benkyō ga hakadorazu karikari shite 'ru.

My big sister's so uptight 'cause she's gotta take entrance exams pretty soon and she's havin' trouble studying.

katto naru/suru (カッとなる／する) "to flare up" V See red, hit the ceiling, lose one's head.

犯人は被害者に借金を断られ、カッとなって首を絞めたらしい。

Hannin wa higai-sha ni shakkin o kotowarare, katto natte kubi o shimeta rashii.

It looks like the guy who did it (the murderer) got bent all out of shape and strangled the victim 'cause he refused to lend him some money.

つまらないことでカッとするのはよしてよ。また血圧があがるわ。

Tsumaranai koto de katto suru no wa yoshite yo. Mata ketsuatsu ga agaru wa.

Don't get all worked up over some stupid little thing. Your blood pressure'll go up again.

kusaru (腐る) "to rot" Ⅴ Be soured on life, down in the mouth, bummed out.

そんなに腐るなよ、失敗はだれにだってあることなんだから。

Sonna ni kusaru na yo, shippai wa dare ni datte aru koto nan da kara.

Don't be so down on the world, man. Anybody can make a mistake.

mappira (真っ平) "earnestly" Ａ No way, not on your life, nothing doing.

あんながめつい人にお金を貸すなんて、真っ平だわ。

Anna gametsui hito ni okane o kasu nante, mappira da wa.

You got another think comin' if you think I'm gonna lend money to some greedyguts like him.

☞ Corruption of the much older *mahira*, the original meaning of which is "solely" or "earnestly."

megeru (めげる) Ⅴ **"to become chipped (broken up into pieces)"** Ⅴ Get bummed out, be (get) down, let something get to one.

はっきり嫌いだとか彼女に直接いわれちゃうと、めげるよなあ。

Hakkiri kirai da to ka kanojo ni chokusetsu iwarechau to, megeru yo nā.

I can see how a guy'd take it hard if his girlfriend came right out and said she hated him.

☞ Youth. Used in the expression *megeru yo nā* as an exclamation.

meromero (めろめろ) "to boohoo" Ａ Be all broken up; don't know which end is up, be all screwed up.

一日中上司から文句を言われ続けて、おれはもうメロメロだよ。

Ichinichi-jū jōshi kara monku o iwaretsuzukete, ore wa mō meromero da yo.

I'm just about at the end of my rope what with the boss chewing me out all day long.

munakuso-warui (胸糞悪い) "(my) shitty chest is bad" Ａｄ Sickening, disgusting, pukey.

自分の大切な車を盗まれたこと、思い出しただけでも胸糞悪い。

Jibun no taisetsu na kuruma o nusumareta koto, omoidashita dake de mo munakuso-warui.

It makes me sick (I get all bummed out) just thinking about having had my car ripped off.

☞ *Muna* is a corruption of *mune* (chest), with *kuso* (excrement, shit) added for emphasis.

mushakusha suru (むしゃくしゃする) "to be unkempt" Ⓥ Be fed up, be up to here, have had it.

おれ、競輪で大負けしてむしゃくしゃして工場に放火したんだ。

Ore, keirin de ōmake shite mushakusha shite kōjō ni hōka shita n' da.

I torched the factory because I had just had it with blowing all my money at the bicycle races.

nan no sono (なんのその) "what, (only) that" Ⓐ No sweat, no big deal, don't mean nothin'.

バイクだから、車の渋滞なんかなんのその。スイスイ行けるわ。

Baiku da kara, kuruma no jūtai nanka nan no sono. Suisui ikeru wa.

I ride a bike, so traffic jams are no big deal as far as I'm concerned. I just cruise right on through 'em.

okkana-bikkuri (おっかなびっくり) "awfully surprised" Ⓐd Be a weenie, be a pussy, be shaking all over.

小心者の太郎は、なにをやるにもおっかなびっくりで困るのさ。

Shōshin-mono no Tarō wa, nani o yaru ni mo okkana-bikkuri de komaru no sa.

I don't know what to do with that Taro. He's such a weenie.

☞ *Okkana* is associated with the primary meaning of *okkanai* (terrifying, awesome).

piripiri suru (ピリピリする) "[of pain] to smart" Ⓥ Be on pins and needles, uptight, be a bundle of nerves, on edge.

いま警察は暴力団の抗争事件でピリピリしてるから気をつけな。

Ima keisatsu wa bōryoku-dan no kōsō-jiken de piripiri shite 'ru kara ki o tsukena.

Watch out, the cops are on the lookout because of all the gang violence that's been going on recently.

punpun suru (プンプンする) "to reek" Ⓥ Be pissed off, fuming, steaming, up in arms, bent out of shape.

姉貴は、美容院で変なヘアスタイルにされてプンプンしている。

Aneki wa, biyō-in de hen na heasutairu ni sarete punpun shite iru.

My big sister is ranting and raving because the place where she got her hair done really screwed it up.

runrun suru (ルンルンする) "zippity do da" Ⓥ Be on cloud nine, high, happy as a lark, in seventh heaven.

恋人から指輪をプレゼントされたんで、彼女ルンルンしてるのよ。

Koibito kara yubiwa o purezento sareta n' de, kanojo runrun shite 'ru no yo.

She's tickled pink because she got a ring from her boyfriend.

☞ Nonsense syllables from the television cartoon *Hana no Ko Runrun*. Since circa 1982.

sabasaba suru (サバサバする) "to feel refreshed" Ⓥ Feel like a weight was lifted from one's shoulders.

いやな亭主と別れてサバサバしたわ。これであたしも自由だわ。

Iya na teishu to wakarete sabasaba shita wa. Kore de atashi mo jiyū da wa.

It really feels great to be rid of that asshole husband of mine. Now I can finally spread my wings.

sappari suru (さっぱりする) "to feel purified" Ⓥ Feel great, feel relieved, feel like a new man (woman).

彼に今日、はっきりと交際を断ったの。あたし、とてもさっぱりしたわ。

Kare ni kyō, hakkiri to kōsai o kotowatta no. Atashi, totemo sappari shita wa.

I broke up with him today, and it feels great.

tamageru (たまげる) "to be scared spiritless" Ⓥ Be flabbergasted, blown away, bowled over, stunned.

突然どなられたら、いくら冷静なあいつだってたまげる。

Totsuzen donararetara, ikura reisei na aitsu datte tamageru.

I don't care how laid back you are, you'd blow your cool if someone laid into you all of a sudden.

☞ From a blending of the words *tama* (魂; soul or spirit), and *geru* (消る), a corruption of the verb *kieru* (disappear).

yake ni naru (やけになる) "to become burned" Ⓥ Be desperate, freak out, go ape, go bananas, lose one's bearings.

女にフラれたぐらいでやけになるな。またいい人に巡り合うさ。

Onna ni furareta gurai de yake ni naru na. Mata ii hito ni meguriau sa.

Don't let getting dumped by some bitch do a job on you. You'll find yourself another woman.

yakeppachi (やけっぱち) **"burned bowl"** N Don't give a shit, couldn't care less.

惚れた女にフラれて、オレはやけっぱちになって旅に出たんだ。

*Horeta onna ni furarete, ore wa yakeppachi ni natte tabi ni deta n'
da.*

My woman gave me my walkin' papers, so I figured what the hell, I
might as well take off on a trip.

☞ Emphatic form of *yake* (see preceding entry), made by blending *yake* (焼け;
burned) and the *hachi* (bowl) of the synonymous *sutebachi* (chucked bowl).

zokkon (ぞっこん) **"from the bottom of the roots"** A In love,
crazy about, be so in love that one can't see straight.

一目見た瞬間から、おれは彼女にぞっこんなんだ。結婚したい!

*Hitome mita shunkan kara, ore wa kanojo ni zokkon nan da. Kekkon
shitai!*

I was a goner the minute I laid eyes on her. I wanna marry that
woman!

☞ Corruption of *sokkon* (底根; bottom root).

The World Around Us:
Red Marks, Skid Stoppers, and the Four Biggies

akaten (赤点) "red mark" N Failing grade, an F.

今度の数学の試験で59点以下のやつは、赤点だから落第だぞ。

Kondo no sūgaku no shiken de gojūkyū-ten ika no yatsu wa, akaten da kara rakudai da zo.

Everybody who gets less than 60 on the math test this time fails. Got that?

☞ From the practice of writing failing grades in red on report cards and the like.

anchoko (あんちょこ) "eezy" N Study guide, crib, pony.

アンチョコを見たって、この物理の問題は解けやしないわ。

Anchoko o mita tte, kono butsuri no mondai wa toke ya shinai wa.

You'll never ever be able to work out this physics problem just by looking at some study guide.

☞ Student use. Corruption of *anchoku* (安直), which means (besides "cheap") to make short, *easy* work of something.

arigane (あり金) "money (that one) has" N Every penny one has (on one), money on hand.

あり金はたいて、彼女の住むリスボン行きの航空券を買ったよ。

Arigane hataite, kanojo no sumu Risubon-yuki no kōkū-ken o katta yo.

He shelled out (forked over, coughed up) all the money he had to buy a ticket to Lisbon, where she was living.

asuko (あすこ) "over thataway" N There, over there, over yonder.

おい、田口。あすこまで駆けっこしないか。おれダッシュには自信あるんだ。

Oi, Taguchi. Asuko made kakekko shinai ka. Ore dasshu ni wa jishin aru n' da.

Hey, Taguchi! Race you as far as that there spot. I'm pretty good at short distances.

☞ Corruption of *asoko.*

binibon (ビニ本) "vinyl book" N A girlie mag, a dirty magazine, a fuck book.

弟の部屋を掃除していたら、ビニ本が枕の下に隠してあったのよ。

Otōto no heya o sōji shite itara, binibon ga makura no shita ni kaku-shite atta no yo.

I found one of those dirty magazines under my little brother's pillow when I was cleaning his room.

☞ Shortened from *binīru-bon*, such magazines being sealed in plastic (*binīru*, Japanese pronunciation of vinyl) to prevent people from thumbing through them at bookstores. Since 1980.

biri (びり) **"hindmost"** Ⓝ The tail end, the ass end, last, (bring up) the rear.

高校のときの成績はビリだった。

Kōkō no toki no seiseki wa biri datta.

I was at the bottom of my class in high school.

boro (ぼろ) **"rag"** Ⓝ Shortcoming, defect, dirt, one's bad side.

初めてのデートなのについ大声で笑って、彼の前でボロ出しちゃったの。

Hajimete no dēto na no ni tsui ōgoe de waratte, kare no mae de boro dashichatta no.

I showed my true colors by laughing like a hyena when we were out on our first date.

butabako (ブタ箱) **"pig box"** Ⓝ Jail, the can, the cooler, the clink.

前科者のおまえがまた捕まったら、ブタ箱行きは確実だからな。

Zenka-mono no omae ga mata tsukamattara, butabako-yuki wa kaku-jitsu da kara na.

Guy with a record like you've got, they'll lock you up next time for sure.

☞ Used among criminals and law enforcement officers.

charinko (ちゃりんこ) **"bike"** Ⓝ Bicycle, bike.

今度買うチャリンコは、絶対ビーチ・クルーザーにするつもりだ。

Kondo kau charinko wa, zettai bīchi-kurūzā ni suru tsumori da.

Next bike I buy's definitely gonna be a beach cruiser.

☞ Also *chari*. The meaning does not include "motorcycle."

choko (チョコ) Ⓝ Chocolate, a chocolate bar, a candy bar.

あたしの姉貴は、甘いチョコより苦いチョコのほうが好きね。

Atashi no aneki wa, amai choko yori nigai choko no hō ga suki ne.

My big sister likes bittersweet chocolate better than the sweet stuff.

chūkin (駐禁) **"stopping forbidden"** Ⓝ No parking.

ここは駐禁だから、車を止めるとすぐに警察がやってきますよ。

Koko wa chūkin da kara, kuruma o tomeru to sugu ni keisatsu ga yatte kimasu yo.

This is a no-parking zone. Leave it here and the cops'll be right around.
☞ Abbreviation of *chūsha-kinshi*.

daimyō-ryokō (大名旅行) "daimyo journey" N Junket, excursion.

議員さんたちの海外視察は、大名旅行で税金の無駄遣いだよな。

Giin-san–tachi no kaigai-shisatsu wa, daimyō-ryokō de zeikin no muda-zukai da yo na.

These overseas fact-finding tours that Diet members go galavanting off on are really just junkets that waste the taxpayer's money, don'cha think?
☞ The entry word refers to the journey that feudal lords in the Tokugawa period were required to make from their outlying fiefs to the shogun's capital of Edo.

dokka (どっか) "somewheres" N Somewhere, anywhere, someplace.

麻布あたりでおいしいミャンマー料理の店、どっか知らないか？

Azabu-atari de oishii Myanmā-ryōri no mise, dokka shiranai ka?

Where's a good Burmese restaurant around Azabu, you know?
☞ Corruption of *doko ka*.

donkō (鈍行) "dull going" N The slow train, local (train).

この年末は、おれはお金がないから鈍行で故郷に帰るしかない。

Kono nenmatsu wa, ore wa okane ga nai kara donkō de kokyō ni kaeru shika nai.

I'm scraping the bottom of the barrel, so it looks like I'll have to make the trip back home (back to my folks' place, back to the old homestead) this New Year's on a local.
☞ A colloquial coinage in antithesis to *kyūkō*.

Ei-bī-shī-dī (A・B・C・D) N A: kiss, suck face, get to first base; B: make out, neck, get some titty, cop a feel, feel up, get to second base (also finger-fuck, get to third base); C: score, fuck, get to home base; D: get pregnant, knock up.

初めて会った男といきなりＣはまずいね。やっぱりＡからだよ。

Hajimete atta otoko to ikinari shī wa mazui ne. Yappari ei kara da yo.

Jumping in bed with some guy you just met's goin' a little too fast. Kissin's alright, though.

まだＢぐらいまでかと思ったら、もうあいつらＤなんだって。

Mada bī gurai made ka to omottara, mō aitsu-ra dī nan datte.

She's already knocked up and here I was thinking they were still

just suckin' face and neckin'.
☞ Student use.

famikon (ファミコン) Ⓝ A video game, a Nintendo.

徹夜でファミコンなんかしていて大丈夫なの？試験に落ちるわ。

Tetsuya de famikon nanka shite ite daijōbu na no? Shiken ni ochiru wa.

Do you know what you're doing, staying up all night playing Nintendo? You'll flunk the test, you know.
☞ An abbreviation of *famirī-conpyūtā* (family computer).

gakusai (学祭) "school festival" Ⓝ School festival.

学祭は学生のイベントなのに、なんで先公が企画を決めるんだろう？

Gakusai wa gakusei no ibento na no ni, nande senkō ga kikaku o kimeru n' darō?

The school festival's supposed to be for students, so what are the damn teachers doing deciding everything?
☞ Shortened form of *daigakusai* or *gakuensai*.

gakushoku (学食) "student food" Ⓝ School cafeteria.

学食のメシは安いけど、どれもまずくて食えたもんじゃないぜ。

Gakushoku no meshi wa yasui kedo, dore mo mazukute kueta mon ja nai ze.

The school cafeteria may be cheap, but who can eat that slop?
☞ Shortened form of *gakusei-shokudō*.

gakuwari (学割) "student rate" Ⓝ Student discount.

新幹線で京都までなら、学割を使えば２割引きになるはずですよ。

Shinkan-sen de Kyōto made nara, gakuwari o tsukaeba niwari-biki ni naru hazu desu yo.

You ought to be able to get twenty percent off on a Shinkansen ticket to Kyoto if you use your student discount.
☞ Shortened from *gakusei-waribiki.*

gentsuki (原付き) "motor attached" Ⓝ A 50cc motorcycle (motorbike, scooter, moped).

原付きでも、メットは必ずかぶるようにしなければ危険だね。

Gentsuki de mo, metto wa kanarazu kaburu yō ni shinakereba kiken da ne.

You're just asking for it if you don't wear a helmet even if you're just on a fifty.
☞ Shortened from *gendōki-tsuki jitensha* (原動機付き自転車), or motorized bicycle, now applied to all 50 cc motorcycles and scooters, with *gendōki* meaning "motor." *Metto* is *herumetto.*

gēsen (ゲーセン) Ⓝ Video arcade, game arcade.

池袋のゲーセンには、どんなゲームも揃ってて楽しいらしいよ。

Ikebukuro no gēsen ni wa, donna gēmu mo sorotte 'te tanoshii rashii yo.

There's a far-out video arcade in Ikebukuro that's supposed to have all the hot games.

☞ Among children and teenagers. Shortened from *gēmusentā* (game center).

girichoko (義理チョコ) **"duty chocolate"** Ⓝ Chocolate given on Valentine's Day out of a sense of duty (rather than affection), usually to a woman's male coworkers or boss.

今年のバレンタインデーは、義理チョコを3個もらっただけだぜ。

Kotoshi no barentaindē wa, girichoko o sanko moratta dake da ze.

All I got this Valentine's Day was three perfunctory boxes of chocolate.

☞ It is customary in Japan on Valentine's Day for women to give chocolate to men they like. *Girichoko*, however, is given to maintain good relations with men at a woman's workplace and in no way suggests affection. On March 14, "White Day," the favor is supposed to be returned—a custom less well established.

gotōbi (五十日) **"5 & 10 days"** Ⓝ Days of the month ending in five or zero, traditionally days of clearing accounts and collecting money.

今日は月末で五十日だから、交通渋滞はかなりひどいだろう。

Kyō wa getsumatsu de gotōbi da kara, kōtsū-jūtai wa kanari hidoi darō.

The roads are really going to be crowded today because it's the end of the month and a collection day to boot.

☞ The fifth, tenth, fifteenth, twentieth, twenty-fifth and thirtieth of each month.

hajikko (はじっこ) **"the very edge"** Ⓝ The (tail) end, the back, the tip.

いつもあの子は喫茶店のはじっこの席で、ぼくを待ってるんだ。

Itsumo ano ko wa kissa-ten no hajikko no seki de, boku o matte 'ru n' da.

That chick always sits in the back of the coffee shop and waits for me.

☞ Also *hasshiko*. The standard word is *hashi* (端).

hana-kin (ハナキン／花金) **"flower Friday"** Ⓝ T.G.I.F. (Thank God It's Friday), party time.

ハナキンで、飲みに行こうと思ったら、急に残業を命じられた。

Hanakin de, nomi ni ikō to omottara, kyū ni zangyō o meijirareta.

There I was all hyped 'cause it was Friday and I was gonna party when they laid this overtime on me. / It being Friday, I was all set to go out drinking when they up and said I had to work overtime.

☞ Abbreviated from *hana no Kin'yō-bi*. Slang term for Friday used among younger people who have Saturday and Sunday off.

hikarimono (光もの) "shining things" Ⓝ

1. Fish like mackerel, shad, or whiting whose scales reflect bluish light and are eaten as sushi.

部長は寿司屋に行くと、いつだって光ものしか食べない。

Buchō wa sushi-ya ni iku to, itsu datte hikarimono shika tabenai.

All the boss ever eats when he goes to a sushi shop is mackerel or shad.

2. Flashy clothes.

君が光ものを着てると、水商売の人みたいに見えるんだ。

Kimi ga hikarimono o kite 'ru to, mizu-shōbai no hito mitai ni mieru n' da.

You look like you oughta be workin' in a bar or something when you dress up in those flashy clothes of yours.

hīru (ヒール) Ⓝ High-heels, heels.

会社ではヒールを履いてるけど、本当はスニーカーが好きなの。

Kaisha de wa hīru o haite 'ru kedo, hontō wa sunīkā ga suki na no.

I may wear heels at work, but tennies (sneakers) are really more my style.
☞ Shortened from *haihīru*. Used by women.

honmei (本命) "main destiny" Ⓝ

1. The school, company, etc. one wants to get into most, one's first choice.

本命は東大だけど、すべったらどっかの私大に行けばいい。

Honmei wa Tōdai da kedo, subettara dokka no shidai ni ikeba ii.

I'm aiming for Tokyo University, but I'll go to some private school if I don't make it there.

2. [Coed use] the guy one really wants to marry or go out with.

松野君の友人と付き合っているけど、本命は松野君なの。

Matsuno-kun no yūjin to tsukiatte iru kedo, honmei wa Matsuno-kun na no.

I'm going out with one of Matsuno's friends, but he's the one I really like (have my eye on).
☞ From usage among horse and bicycle enthusiasts to refer to the entry most likely to win, or the favorite. Originally, in Yin-Yang astrology the word refers to the star under which one was born, the one that determines one's destiny.

hōshi (奉仕) "(voluntary) service" Ⓝ Special (price).

こちらのエアコンは、ご奉仕価格で定価の半額になっています。

Kochira no eakon wa, gohōshi-kakaku de teika no hangaku ni natte imasu.

The air-conditioner here is on special for half price.

hotto (ホット) Ⓝ (Hot) coffee.

ねえちゃん、おれにホットひとつとミックスサンドくれるかい？

Nē-chan, ore ni hotto hitotsu to mikkusu-sando kureru kai?

Hey there cutie, how 'bout bringing me a cup of coffee and the mixed sandwich plate.

imantoko (今んとこ) "the present juncture" Ⓝ Right now, for the moment.

去年知り合った彼女とは、今んとこなんとかうまくいってるよ。

Kyonen shiriatta kanojo to wa, imantoko nan to ka umaku itte 'ru yo.

For the time being (as things stand now) I'm getting along pretty well with the girl I met last year.

☞ Corruption of *ima no tokoro* (at the present place [in time]).

itchō (一丁) "one game" Ⓝ One, once; a shot, a go.

おまえと会うの、久しぶりだなあ。一丁飲みにでもいかないか。

Omae to au no, hisashiburi da nā. Itchō nomi ni de mo ikanai ka.

Jeez, long time no see, huh. Whadaya say we have a drink?

☞ Used to introduce a comment suggesting doing something. Originally a counter for various things, the meaning here is probably derived from its use in counting matches or competitive games.

itchōra (一張羅) "one suit of silk" Ⓝ One's Sunday-go-to-meeting clothes, one's best clothes, one's good clothes.

今日は初めてのデートだし、一張羅のスーツを着ていこうかな。

Kyō wa hajimete no dēto da shi, itchōra no sūtsu o kite ikō ka na.

First date with her today; hell, I might as well dress up in my best suit for the occasion.

jījan (ジージャン) Ⓝ A jean jacket, a denim jacket, a Levis jacket.

結婚式に行くのに、ジージャン着てっちゃまずいんじゃないの。

Kekkon-shiki ni iku no ni, jījan kite 'tcha mazui n' ja nai no.

Don't you think it's a little weird to go to a wedding in a jean jacket?

☞ Portmanteau from English "jean" and "jumper."

jīpan (ジーパン) Ⓝ Jeans, Levis.

Ｇパンをはくんだったら、やっぱり501が一番カッコいいよ。

Jīpan o haku n' dattara, yappari gō-maru-ichi ga ichiban kakko ii yo.

When it comes to jeans, 501s look the sharpest.

☞ Portmanteau from English "jeans" and "pants." Commonly written with a capital "G."

karaoke (カラオケ／空オケ) "empty orchestra" N Karaoke.

兄貴は、毎晩スナックへ行って、カラオケで歌ってばかりいる。

Aniki wa, maiban sunakku e itte, karaoke de utatte bakari iru.

All my older brother ever does is go to karaoke bars every night and sing.

☞ *Oke* is the shortened form of *ōkesutora* (orchestra). Since 1977 when it was first popularized in Osaka.

karimen (仮免) "provisional license" N A learner's permit; a temporary license.

今日仮免が取れたら、もうすぐ彼とドライブに行けるんだわ。

Kyō karimen ga toretara, mō sugu kare to doraibu ni ikeru n' da wa.

If I get my learner's permit today, it shouldn't be long before I can go for a drive with my boyfriend.

☞ Abbreviated form of *karimen-kyō* or *karimen-jō*.

kone (コネ) N Connection(s), pull.

ぼくはこの会社に専務のコネで入ったから、試験は受けていない。

Boku wa kono kaisha ni senmu no kone de haitta kara, shiken wa ukete inai.

I got into the company through the managing director, so I didn't have to take the test.

役所の担当者にコネをつけて、うちの製品を売り込みたいもんだ。

Yakusho no tantō-sha ni kone o tsukete, uchi no seihin o urikomitai mon da.

I wanna try to sell our company's products by going through someone in charge of that sort of thing at city hall.

☞ Abbreviated form of English "connection."

konpa (コンパ) N A party, a mixer.

今度の金曜日は京大の人たちとコンパで盛り上がる予定なの。

Kondo no Kin'yō-bi wa Kyōdai no hitotachi to konpa de moriagaru yotei na no.

We're gonna party on down with some people from Kyoto University this Friday.

☞ From the English "company" insofar as it means those one associates with. Used by students.

maihōmu (マイホーム) N One's own house (home).

都心にマイホームを持つなんて、サラリーマンには無理な夢だ。

Toshin ni maihōmu o motsu nante, sararīman ni wa muri na yume da.

Owning one's own home in the center of town is a pipedream for most office workers these days.

あいつはマイホーム主義だから、残業は一切したがらないんだ。

Aitsu wa maihōmu-shugi da kara, zangyō wa issai shitagaranai n' da.

He's a real family man, so he refuses to stick around and work over-time.

☞ Japanese English "my home."

mekkemono (めっけもの) "a thing found" N A real find.

バーゲンで買った服、ミッソーニだったの。めっけものだった。

Bāgen de katta fuku, Missōni datta no. Mekkemono datta.

I lucked out when I picked up some clothes that were Missoni at a sale. What a find!

☞ *Mekke* comes from the verb *mekkeru*, a corruption of *mitsukeru*.

mentē (免停) "license suspended" N Suspension of one's (driver's) license.

佐藤君は飲酒運転で捕まって免停になったから、今は運転できないんだ。

Satō-kun wa inshu-unten de tsukamatte mentē ni natta kara, ima wa unten dekinai n' da.

Sato got picked up on a D.W.I. (Driving While Intoxicated) and had his license pulled, so he can't drive now.

☞ Shortened from *menkyō-teishi*. *Tē* is a corruption of *tei*.

mesen (目線) "eye line" N A look, one's eyes.

あたしがディスコで踊るとき、いつも男の熱い目線を感じるの。

Atashi ga disuko de odoru toki, itsumo otoko no atsui mesen o kan-jiru no.

I always get this feeling that guys are scoping (checking) me out when I'm dancing at a disco.

meshi (メシ) "(cooked) rice" N Something to eat, food, a meal, chow, chop.

君は外でメシを食うのかい、それとも自分で料理するのかい。

Kimi wa soto de meshi o kuu no kai, sore to mo jibun de ryōri suru no kai.

You eat out or cook for yourself at home?

☞ Male usage.

mōningu (モーニング) N The breakfast special (at coffee shops etc.).

午前11時までなら、喫茶店で安いモーニングが食べられるよ。

Gozen jūichi-ji made nara, kissa-ten de yasui mōningu ga taberareru yo.

You can usually get a breakfast special pretty cheap at a coffee

shop until about eleven.
☞ From the English "morning."

natsumero (懐メロ) "nostalgic melody" Ⓝ An oldie but goodie, golden oldie.

あいつまだ若いくせに、カラオケでは懐メロばっかり歌うんだ。

Aitsu mada wakai kuse ni, karaoke de wa natsumero bakkari utau n' da.

For a young guy, he sure sings a lota oldies when he goes to a karaoke bar.
☞ From the radio program *Natsukashi no Merodī* (Nostalgic Melodies).

negura (ねぐら) "(bird's) roost" Ⓝ One's place, pad, digs.

太郎はアパートが見つかるまで、おれの部屋をねぐらにしてた。

Tarō wa apāto ga mitsukaru made, ore no heya o negura ni shite 'ta.

Taro was putting up at my place till he found an apartment of his own.

nekku (ネック) Ⓝ The rub, a bottleneck.

女性問題がネックになってね、奥松君の係長昇格は延期になったよ。

Josei-mondai ga nekku ni natte ne, Okumatsu-kun no kakari-chō–shōkaku wa enki ni natta yo.

Okumatsu's promotion to section chief hit a snag over his womanizing.
☞ From the English "bottleneck."

neta (ネタ) "eedsay" Ⓝ [Information] poop, skinny, lowdown, dirt, (inside) dope; [proof] the goods.

芸能記者の兄貴は、ネタになる話を探して一日中歩き回っている。

Geinō-kisha no aniki wa, neta ni naru hanashi o sagashite ichinichi-jū arukimawatte iru.

My older brother's a reporter who has to cover the stars, so he's always beating the pavement trying to get a scoop.

おい、ネタはあがってるんだ！素直に罪を認めたらどうなんだ。

Oi, neta wa agatte 'ru n' da! Sunao ni tsumi o mitometara dō nan da.

We've got the shit on you! Whaddaya say ya just come clean, huh.
☞ Inverted reading of *tane* (seed), for which the literal English meaning above is pig Latin. Originally used by hucksters and hoodlums.

ofisu-rabu (オフィスラブ) Ⓝ A love affair with a coworker, esp. between a married man in a supervisory position and a younger woman employee.

直美と部長のオフィスラブのことは、まだだれも気づいてない。

Naomi to buchō no ofisu-rabu no koto wa, mada dare mo kizuite 'nai.

Nobody's got wind yet of the hanky-panky going on between Naomi and the department head.

☞ From English-sounding Japanese coinage "office love."

ohiya (お冷) "chills" N

1. (Cold) water [served in restaurants and coffee shops].

おばさん、すみませんけど、お冷をもう一杯いただけませんか？

Obasan, sumimasen kedo, ohiya o mō ippai itadakemasen ka?

Excuse me. Could I have another glass of water, please, ma'am?

2. Cold rice.

あんた帰ってくるのが遅かったから、もうお冷しかないわよ。

Anta kaette kuru no ga osokatta kara, mō ohiya shika nai wa yo.

Since you're so late getting home, all that's left is cold rice.

omanma (おまんま) "goodie goodie" N Rice, food.

おれが稼いでるおかげで、おまえらはおまんま食ってるんだぞ。

Ore ga kaseide 'ru okage de, omae-ra wa omanma kutte 'ru n' da zo.

How do you think this food gets on the table, anyway?

☞ Vulgar. Most likely derived, through contracted *mama*, from the childish *uma-uma* (a repetition of what is now *umai*, or "good tasting"). The word is standard as baby talk.

onamida-chōdai (お涙ちょうだい) "give me tears" A tearjerker.

この懐メロ、お涙ちょうだいだとわかっていても泣けちゃうわ。

Kono natsumero, onamida-chōdai da to wakatte ite mo nakechau wa.

I know this oldie's meant to be a tearjerker, but I still can't help crying every time I hear it.

pansuto (パンスト) N Pantyhose.

いくら暑くても、パンストはかないで会社には行かれないのよ。

Ikura atsukute mo, pansuto hakanai de kaisha ni wa ikarenai no yo.

It doesn't matter how hot it is, I can't very well go to work without wearing stockings.

☞ Used by women. From Japanese coinage "panty stocking."

pasokon (パソコン) N Personal computer, PC.

パソコンと聞いただけで敬遠するおじんが多いから困るね。

Pasokon to kiita dake de keien suru ojin ga ōi kara komaru ne.

Trouble is, all you have to do is mention the word "personal computer" and a lot of older guys start backing off.

☞ Shortened from *pasonaru konpyūtā*.

pokke (ポッケ) N Pocket.

坊や、ポッケの中にカエルなんか入れちゃだめじゃない。死んじゃう
わよ。

*Bōya, pokke no naka ni kaeru nanka irecha dame ja nai. Shinjau wa
yo.*

Better not put that froggy in your pocket, little fella. It'll die.

☞ Diminutive use by small children of the English "pocket" (ポケット).

ponkotsu (ぽんこつ) "fist" N Junk, a wreck; [of a car] a junker.

去年3万円で買ったポンコツのスバルが、壊れて動かなくなった。

*Kyonen san-man'en de katta ponkotsu no Subaru ga, kowarete ugo-
kanaku natta.*

You know that Subaru I picked up for thirty thousand yen last year?
Well, the junker finally gave up the ghost.

☞ Original meaning seems to have been to hit with the fist, or to hit and kill (i.e.,
to slaughter animals).

raji-kase (ラジカセ) N A (portable) radio-cassette stereo, a boom
box, a ghetto blaster.

あたしは海岸に寝そべって、ラジカセでサザンを聴くのが好き。

Atashi wa kaigan ni nesobette, raji-kase de Sazan o kiku no ga suki.

I like relaxing on the beach and listening to the Southern Allstars on
my boom box.

☞ Shortened form of *rajio-kasetto* (radio-cassette).

rikurūto-katto (リクルートカット) "Recruit cut" N A short
haircut, a cropped look supposed to impress prospective employers.

長髪をリクルートカットにしたら、会社訪問の準備は完了だね。

*Chōhatsu o Rikurūto-katto ni shitara, kaisha-hōmon no junbi wa
kanryō da ne.*

Once I get my ears raised, I'll be all set to make the rounds of some
prospective employers.

☞ From the employment information magazine *Rikurūto* (Recruit).

sakippo (さきっぽ／先っぽ) "tippy end" N Tip, top, end.

弟が、ぼくのエッフェル塔の模型のさきっぽを折っちゃったよ。

Otōto ga, boku no Efferu-tō no mokei no sakippo o otchatta yo.

My little brother broke the tip off my model of the Eiffel Tower.

☞ Colloquialization of *saki*.

sarakin (サラ金) "salary finance" N Loan shark.

サラ金で5万円借りただけなのに、4万円も利息を請求された。

*Sarakin de go-man'en karita dake na no ni, yon-man'en mo risoku o
seikyū sareta.*

Borrowed a measly fifty thousand yen from a loan shark and now
they want forty thousand yen in interest alone.

☞ Shortened from *sararīman-kin'yū*, or financial (services for) office workers.

saten (茶店) "T shop" N Coffee shop.

さっき茶店でコーヒー飲んだら、ウェーターは知り合いだった。

Sakki saten de kōhī nondara, uētā wa shiriai datta.

I bumped into some guy I knew who was waiting tables at this coffee
shop I was just in.

☞ Students and young people. Shortened from *kissa-ten*.

sekohan (セコハン) N Secondhand, used.

今度買ったセコハンのヴェスパは、けっこう調子よくて快適だよ。

*Kondo katta sekohan no Vesupa wa, kekkō chōshi yokute kaiteki da
yo.*

The Vespa I picked up secondhand this time is great. It runs pretty
smooth.

☞ Transliterated and shortened from English "secondhand."

shaba (シャバ／娑婆) "the world of endurance of suffering" N

Normal life as viewed from prison or the military, the world; civilian
life.

あと半年で刑期も終わりかあ。早くシャバの空気が吸いてえなあ。

*Ato han-toshi de keiki mo owari kā. Hayaku shaba no kūki ga suitē
nā.*

Six months more and I'll be outa stir. Can't wait to get back out in
the world.

☞ From Buddhism. Originally meaning the human world as a realm of suffering
and the endurance of suffering; that is, the normal human world.

shakai no mado (社会の窓) "social window" N One's fly, barn
door.

見ろ！あのオヤジ、社会の窓が開いてパンツがまる見えだぜ。

Miro! Ano oyaji, shakai no mado ga aite pantsu ga maru-mie da ze.

Check out that old fart! Barn door's wide open and you can see his
shorts.

shiromono (代物) "merchandise" N Thing, sucker, mother,
bugger.

通信販売で買った包丁は、粗悪品で本当にひどい代物だったわ。

*Tsūshin-hanbai de katta hōchō wa, soaku-hin de hontō ni hidoi
shiromono datta wa.*

That kitchen knife I got through the mail was a real piece of junk.

先週末にこのキャバレーにホステスとして入った女性は、たいした代

物だぜ、だんな。

*Senshū-matsu ni kono kyabarē ni hosutesu toshite haitta josei wa,
taishita shiromono da ze, danna.*

You oughta get an eyeful of the babe that started hostessing here last
weekend, bub. She's really something.

☞ Originally used about something being sold or its price. Now used about both
people and things, it often suggests inferiority or contempt.

suberidome (すべりどめ) "skid stopper" Ⓝ A school one applies
to just in case one isn't accepted elsewhere.

すべりどめに受けた大学まですべったから、浪人しかないんだ。

*Suberidome ni uketa daigaku made subetta kara, rōnin shika nai n'
da.*

Failed the entrance exam for the school I was counting on, so gotta
spend another year studying and try again.

☞ Students.

suka (すか) "dupe" Ⓝ A miss, flop, dud, loser; a losing (lottery)
ticket.

このスイカは甘いと思って買ったのにまたスカを食った。

Kono suika wa amai to omotte katta no ni mata suka o kutta.

I thought for sure this watermelon was gonna be sweet when I
bought it, but no way, Jose.

この映画、絶対おもしろいと期待して観たけれどスカだったね。

Kono eiga, zettai omoshiroi to kitai shite mita keredo suka datta ne.

I was lookin' forward to this being a great flick, but it turned out to
be a major disaster.

☞ From the old verb *sukasu* (dupe).

sunpō (寸法) "measurements" Ⓝ The plan, the way we'll do it,
how it goes.

おまえが店員と話してるすきに、おれが指輪を盗むって寸法さ。

*Omae ga ten'in to hanashite 'ru suki ni, ore ga yubiwa o nusumu tte
sunpō sa.*

Here's how it goes: I'll swipe the ring while you keep the clerk busy
talking.

近所の日焼けサロンで焼いて、ハワイ帰りのふりをするという寸法さ。

*Kinjo no hiyake-saron de yaite, Hawai-gaeri no furi o suru to iu sun-
pō sa.*

Get a tan at some tanning salon in town, then make like he just came
back from Hawaii, that's the way he's going to work it.

tanma (たんま) "imetay" Ⓝ Time (out).

ちょっと、タンマ。鬼が誰か、みんなわかってやってるのかい。

Chotto, tanma. Oni ga dare ka, minna wakatte yatte 'ru no kai.

Time out! You guys know who's "it"?

☞ Possibly an inversion of *matta*, or "wait." Used among children. Literal meaning here is pig Latin.

tanpan (短パン) Ⓝ Shorts, cutoffs.

オリエンタルホテルでは、短パンをはいてると中に入れないよ。

Orientaru-hoteru de wa, tanpan o haite 'ru to naka ni hairenai yo.

They won't let you in the Oriental Hotel if you're wearing shorts.

☞ From the character for "short," *tan*, and *pan*, from the Japanese pronunciation of "pants" (*pantsu*).

usoppachi (うそっぱち) "a big fat lie" Ⓝ A whopper, a line of crap, bullshit.

ねえ、由美。社員旅行なんてうそっぱちで、ほかの男と温泉に行って
たんだろう？

Nē, Yumi. Shain-ryokō nante usoppachi de, hoka no otoko to onsen ni itte 'ta n' darō?

You're lying through your teeth (just feeding me a line of crap) about being on a company outing, aren't you, Yumi? You really went off to some hot spring with another guy, right?

☞ Stronger than the normal word for lie, *uso* (嘘).

yondai (四大) "four biggies" Ⓝ A four-year college, a university.

最近は、短大よりも四大に進む女のほうが多いんだってね。

Saikin wa, tandai yori mo yondai ni susumu onna no hō ga ōi n' datte ne.

From what I hear, more women are going to four-year schools now than jaycees.

☞ Similar shortened forms include *tandai* for *tanki-daigaku* or junior college (as above), and *joshidai* for *joshi-daigaku* or women's college.

Nature and All That:
The Reel's End and One for a Roll

abekobe (あべこべ) **"topsy-turvy"** Ⓐ All turned around, the other way around, screwed up.

本当の住所は2—5なのに名刺はあべこべに5—2になってた。

Hontō no jūsho wa ni-no-go na no ni meishi wa abekobe ni go-no-ni ni natte 'ta.

The address on my business card was supposed to be 2-5, but they got it assbackwards and wrote it 5-2.

amai (甘い) **"sweet"** Ⓐ

1. Unrealistic, too rosy; slack, lax; lenient, indulgent, permissive.

勉強しないで大学に合格しようなんて甘い考えは捨ててしまえ。

Benkyō shinai de daigaku ni gōkaku shiyō nante amai kangae wa sutete shimae.

You'd better stop kidding yourself, thinking you can get into college without studying.

2. Loose.

ねじが甘いから、この看板はすぐにはずれてしまうよ。

Neji ga amai kara, kono kanban wa sugu ni hazurete shimau yo.

The screws are so loose that this billboard is always falling down.

aotenjō (青天井) **"blue ceiling"** Ⓝ The sky's the limit, way up there in the clouds.

青天井だった不動産業種の株価も、景気の後退で下げはじめたな。

Aotenjō datta fudōsan-gyōshu no kabuka mo, keiki no kōtai de sage-hajimeta na.

What with the recession and all, even the high-flying real estate stocks have started to come back down to earth.

☞ From the notion of the firmament (*aozora*) as a ceiling (*tenjō*).

arittake (ありったけ) **"all available"** Ⓝ Ⓐⅾ

1. Every bit of; the whole works; the whole shootin' match; lock, stock and barrel.

大量にコピーをとるから、ありったけの用紙を総務からもらおう。

Tairyō ni kopī o toru kara, arittake no yōshi o sōmu kara moraō.

I've got to make so many copies of this stuff I'd better get every last piece of paper they have in general affairs.

2. As ... as possible.

ボールをありったけ遠くに投げて、友達と腕試しをしたんだ。

Bōru o arittake tōku ni nagete, tomodachi to udedameshi o shita n' da.

A friend of mine and I were chucking a ball as far as we could (with all our might) to see who had the strongest arm.

☞ Emphatic form of aritake (有り丈).

asedaku (汗だく) "gushing sweat" N Pouring sweat, stinky.

ジョギングで汗だくになったら、必ずシャワーを浴びなさいね。

Jogingu de asedaku ni nattara, kanarazu shawā o abinasai ne.

Make sure you shower after you come back all sweaty from jogging, okay.

☞ Shortened from *asedakudaku*. *Dakudaku* is mimetic for the gushing forth of such liquids as sweat and blood.

atariki-shariki (あたりきしゃりき) "right as rain" A What do you think, does a cat have an ass, does a bear shit in the woods.

この寿司は旨いかだと？あたりきしゃりきよ。おれが握ったんだ。

Kono sushi wa umai ka da to? Atariki-shariki yo. Ore ga nigitta n' da.

Say what? Is this sushi good? Does a chicken have lips, man? I made it myself.

☞ *Atariki* is a corruption of *atarimae*, which means "obviously," and *shariki* possibly derives from *jinrikisha-fu*, or *rikisha* man. Blended for the repetitive sound of *riki*, there appears to be no special underlying meaning. Used by men.

babatchii (ばばっちい) "icky-poo" A Dirty, filthy, icky, yucky.

たあちゃん、おててばばっちいでしょ。ごはんの前に洗いなさい。

Tā-chan, otete babatchii desho. Gohan no mae ni arainasai.

Your pinkies are all yucky, aren't they, Tā-chan? Let's wash them before we eat, like a good little boy.

☞ From the older *baba*, the childish word for a bowel movement, or poo-poo, made over into an adjective.

bakka (ばっか) "jus'" Ad Only, just.

ママったら、あたしにばっか掃除させて自分はなにもしないのよ。

Mama 'ttara, atashi ni bakka sōji sasete jibun wa nani mo shinai no yo.

You're always making me do all the housework, Mom. You never do any yourself.

新築したばっかのおれの家が、昨日の火事で全焼しちゃった。

Shinchiku shita bakka no ore no ie ga, kinō no kaji de zenshō shi-chatta.

The fire yesterday burned down my brand-new house (the house I
jus' built).
☞ Colloquial corruption of *bakari*.

baribari (ばりばり) "ripping" Ⓐ Ⓐd Hard-working, hard-driving, enthusiastic.

鈴木は、ばりばり仕事をする部下を嫌う変わった人物なんだ。

*Suzuki wa, baribari shigoto o suru buka o kirau kawatta jinbutsu nan
da.*

Suzuki's weird the way he doesn't like people under him who are
really into their work.
☞ From the onomatopoetic word for the sound of something like cloth being torn,
or the sound made when one bites into something crisp.

batan-kyū (バタンキュー) "plunk–phew" Ⓐ Be completely exhausted and go to bed, wasted and sack out, crash and burn.

昨日のサッカーの猛練習で、家に帰ったらバタンキューだった。

Kinō no sakkā no mō-renshū de, ie ni kaettara batan-kyū datta.

Soccer practice was so hard yesterday that I just crashed the second I
got home.
☞ Blend of *batan*, onomatopoetic for something heavy falling with a dull thud,
and *kyū*, onomatopoetic for the groan one involuntarily emits when under attack or
pressure.

batchiri (ばっちり) "bang" Ⓐd Right on, no sweat, A-Okay.

面接試験で予想どおりの質問が出たから、ばっちり答えちゃった。

*Mensetsu-shiken de yosō-dōri no shitsumon ga deta kara, batchiri
kotaechatta.*

The interview questions were exactly what I figured they'd be, so I
breezed through it.
☞ Young people.

berabō (べらぼう) "freakish" Ⓐ Outrageous, unheard of.

コーヒー1杯千円なんてそんなべらぼうな金額払えないよ。

Kōhī ippai sen'en nante sonna berabō na kingaku haraenai yo.

A thousand fuckin' yen for a cup of coffee? No way I can pay that.

香港へ日帰りで出張だと？そんなべらぼうな話しは信じられないな。

*Honkon e higaeri de shutchō da to? Sonna berabō na hanashi wa
shinjirarenai na.*

A business trip to Hong Kong and back the same day? You've gotta
be kidding, man.
☞ Thought to be rooted in the Kanbun era (1661-1673), when a dark-skinned,
red-eyed, human monstrosity with facial features resembling a monkey, known
variously as a *berabō* or *bekubō*, was shown in freak shows. Primarily used among
men.

beronberon (べろんべろん) "double-tongued" Ⓐ Blown away, bombed, hammered, plastered, sloshed, shit-faced, wiped out.

バーボン1本を一晩で空にして、べろんべろんに酔っぱらった。

Bābon ippon o hitoban de kara ni shite, beronberon ni yopparatta.

I killed a whole bottle of bourbon the other night and got thoroughly
  smashed.

☞ An emphatic form of *berobero* (roll around with the tongue; get dead drunk).
Bero is colloquial for "tongue."

bichabicha (びちゃびちゃ) "splashed" Ⓐ Soaking (wet), dripping (wet), sopping (wet).

降りしきる雨のなかを傘なしで歩いたから全身びちゃびちゃだ。

Furishikiru ame no naka o kasa-nashi de aruita kara zenshin bicha-bicha da.

I got completely drenched from walking around in a steady rain
  without an umbrella.

☞ Probably associated with *pichapicha*, the sound made by walking through shallow water.

bochibochi (ぼちぼち) "spotty" Ⓐd Slowly, leisurely.

会議は10時からだったね。10分前だし、ぼちぼち行こうか。

Kaigi wa jū-ji kara datta ne. Juppun mae da shi, bochibochi ikō ka.

The meeting's at 10, right? It's ten to now, so maybe we should get a
  move on (start moseying on over there).

☞ Synonymous with *pochipochi* and *botsubotsu*. All three probably derive from
pochi/bochi (a tiny spot or dot).

boroi (ぼろい) "cushy" Ⓐ Well-paying, lucrative, sweet.

1時間働いて1万円くれるなんてボロイ仕事は珍しいよね。

Ichi-jikan hataraite ichi-man'en kureru nante boroi shigoto wa me-zurashii yo ne.

Jobs where you can pull in ten thousand yen an hour are few and far
  between, wouldn't you say.

☞ Associated with *boro-mōke* (clean profit).

boroi (ぼろい) "raggedy" Ⓐ Beat up, worn out.

おれのステレオはボロイから、音がひどくて聴けやしない。

Ore no sutereo wa boroi kara, oto ga hidokute kike ya shinai.

My stereo's not for shit. It sounds so bad I can't stand to listen to it.

☞ Probably derived from *boro* (rag).

chachi (ちゃち) "shoddy" Ⓐ Trashy, sleazy, chintzy, silly, stupid.

古く歴史のある温泉旅館だと聞いて行ってみたら、ちゃちなぼろ宿だった。

Furuku rekishi no aru onsen-ryokan da to kiite itte mitara, chachi na boro-yado datta.

I thought I'd check out this hot spring 'cause I'd heard so much about it being really old and all, but when I got there it turned out just to be some shoddy, run-down place.

こんなちゃちなトリックじゃ、名探偵ホームズでなくても見破れるわね。

Konna chachi na torikku ja, mei-tantei Hōmuzu de nakute mo miya-bureru wa ne.

You don't have to be any Sherlock to see through a stupid trick like this.

chara (ちゃら) **"flam"** N Even-steven, call it even.

君に借りてた5千円、ぼくが食事をおごるからちゃらにしてよ。

Kimi ni karite 'ta go-sen'en, boku ga shokuji o ogoru kara chara ni shite yo.

You know that five thousand yen I owe you? What do you say we call it even if I pick up the dinner tab?

chibichibi (ちびちび) **"itsy-bitsy"** Ad Little by little, bit by bit, in dribs and drabs.

パパは気が滅入ると、ちびちびお酒をのむの。かわいくなっちゃうわ。

Papa wa ki ga meiru to, chibichibi osake o nomu no. Kawaiku nat-chau wa.

It's so cute the way Dad sips away at his sake when he's bummed out about something.

chimachima (ちまちま) **"dinky"** Ad Compressed, compact, crimped, cramped.

あの小説家は、体格がいいのにとてもちまちました字を書くな。

Ano shōsetsu-ka wa, taikaku ga ii no ni totemo chimachima shita ji o kaku na.

For a big guy, that novelist sure writes in a scrunched-up hand.

chinke (ちんけ) **"one snake-eye"** A Crummy, lousy, out of it, the pits.

こんなチンケな場末のバーじゃ、酒を飲む気になれやしない。

Konna chinke na basue no bā ja, sake o nomu ki ni nare ya shinai.

I can't get into doing any serious drinking in a stupid bar out in the sticks like this.

あんなチンケな男にあんた惚れちゃったの。どこがよかったの？

Anna chinke na otoko ni anta horechatta no. Doko ga yokatta no?

You mean to tell me you fell for a scumbag like that guy? What did you ever see in him?

☞ From the word *chin*, which refers to the one on a die.

chinpunkanpun (チンプンカンプン) "gobbledygook" N Non-sense, gibberish, Greek.

パソコンの話は会社のオッサンにはチンプンカンプンらしいよ。

Pasokon no hanashi wa kaisha no ossan ni wa chinpunkanpun rashii yo.

It's all Greek to the old guys in the office when you start talking about computers.

レストラン『フラメンコ』はメニューがスペイン語で書かれていて、ぼくにはチンプンカンプンだった。

Resutoran "Furamenko" wa menyū ga Supein-go de kakarete ite, boku ni wa chinpunkanpun datta.

I couldn't make head or tail out of the menu at the Flamenco because it was all written in Spanish.

chippoke (ちっぽけ) "teensy" Ad Little, tiny, little-bitty, itty-bitty.

ぼくはちっぽけなスーツケースひとつさげてひとり旅にでたんだ。

Boku wa chippoke na sūtsukēsu hitotsu sagete hitori-tabi ni deta n' da.

I went on a trip all by my lonesome, just me and one tiny suitcase.

chobochobo (ちょぼちょぼ) "ditto ditto" Ad
1. Here and there, in splotches, sparsely.

息子も中学生になったら、ひげがちょぼちょぼ生えてきた。

Musuko mo chūgaku-sei ni nattara, hige ga chobochobo haete kita.

My son started getting a few straggly hairs on his chin when he got into junior high.

2. On par with, the same as, six of one and half a dozen of the other, nothing to choose from.

ゴルフの腕前は、あいつもおれもちょぼちょぼで下手だね。

Gorufu no udemae wa, aitsu mo ore mo chobochobo de heta da ne.

We're both just a couple of duffers when it comes to golf, I guess.
☞ From the Japanese equivalent of ditto marks (ゝ), pronounced *chobo*.

choi (ちょい) "a bit" Ad A little, a while, a second.

すぐに支度するから、出かけるのもうちょい待っててくれない？

Sugu ni shitaku suru kara, dekakeru no mō choi matte 'te kurenai?

Would you mind holding on a bit longer? I'll be ready to go in a second.
☞ Shortened from *choi to*, which in turn is probably a curtailment of *chotto*.

choichoi (ちょいちょい) "bit by bit" Ad (Every) now and then.

その人なら、この店にもちょいちょい来るから顔は知ってるわ。

Sono hito nara, kono mise ni mo choichoi kuru kara kao wa shitte 'ru wa.

Oh him? Sure, I know him. He comes in the store (comes here) every so often.

☞ A duplication of *choi*. See note to preceding entry.

chokkiri (ちょっきり) "sharply cut off (with scissors)" Ad Just, right, sharp, exactly.

あのデパートは、いつも10時チョッキリに開店するはずだよ。

Ano depāto wa, itsumo jū-ji chokkiri ni kaiten suru hazu da yo.

That department store should be open at ten sharp.

chokochoko (ちょこちょこ) "pitter-patter" Ad

1. Patter, scurry, scamper; fidget.

坊や、迷子になるからちょこちょこしないでちょうだいよ。

Bōya, maigo ni naru kara chokochoko shinai de chōdai yo.

Hey there, little fella, you'd better quit running around like that or you'll end up getting lost.

岩田は、いつもちょこちょこして落ち着きのない人ね。

Iwata wa, itsumo chokochoko shite ochitsuki no nai hito ne.

Iwata's one antsy guy, the way he's always fidgeting around.

2. All the time, right and left.

最近あいつは、ちょこちょこ学校を休んでバイトしてるね。

Saikin aitsu wa, chokochoko gakkō o yasunde baito shite 'ru ne.

Every time you turn around it seems like he's cutting class to work these days.

☞ Associated by pronunication and the basic meaning of "small" with *chokotto* (same as *chotto*), *chokomaka* (restless, bustling), and *chokonto* (see following entry).

chokonto (ちょこんと) "to bump slightly" Ad

1. Slightly.

池を眺めてたら、鯉がちょこんと水面に顔をだしたんだ。

Ike o nagamete 'tara, koi ga chokonto suimen ni kao o dashita n' da.

A carp poked its head above the surface just as I was looking at the pond.

2. Quietly, like a good boy (girl).

あの子はベンチにちょこんと座って、母親を待っていたわ。

Ano ko wa benchi ni chokonto suwatte, haha-oya o matte ita wa.

The boy was sitting on the bench like a little gentleman waiting for his mother.

choppiri (ちょっぴり) "smidgen" Ad Somewhat, a bit, a pinch.

つい彼につらく当たってしまって、ちょっぴり反省しているの。

Tsui kare ni tsuraku atatte shimatte, choppiri hansei shite iru no.

I laid into him about something and now I'm feeling just a tad guilty about it.

☞ Primarily feminine.

choroi (ちょろい) "lukewarm" A

1. Half-hearted, half-ass(ed).

そんなちょろい方法では、この問題は解けそうにないわね。

Sonna choroi hōhō de wa, kono mondai wa tokesō ni nai wa ne.

You can't expect to solve the problem with some half-baked approach like that, I guess.

2. Piece of cake, no sweat, cake, a cakewalk, easy as pie.

明日の試験はちょろいから、準備する必要はないと思うな。

Ashita no shiken wa choroi kara, junbi suru hitsuyō wa nai to omou na.

Tomorrow's test is gonna be a cinch. Don't see any reason to crack the books.

☞ Young people.

dadappiroi (だだっ広い) "simply spacious" A Wide-open, big, spacious, big and bare, empty.

だだっ広い倉庫は、がらんとしていて一人きりでは怖かった。

Dadappiroi sōko wa, garan to shite ite hitori-kiri de wa kowakatta.

It was scary being all alone in that humongous old empty warehouse.

☞ *Dada* seems to be a corruption of *tada* (only, just, nothing but).

dantotsu (断トツ) "absolutely tops" A N Far better (bigger, richer, etc.), head and shoulders above, in a class by oneself, in a different league, way out in front of the pack.

あいつは猛烈なセールスマンで、売り上げは社内でも断トツさ。

Aitsu wa mōretsu na sērusuman de, uriage wa shanai de mo dantotsu sa.

Dude's one hell of a salesman. He's way out in front of everybody else in the office.

☞ Shortened from *danzen-toppu* (断然トップ).

dasai (ださい) "crappy" A Out of it, not with it, geekish, uncool; square; [of a person's dress] be a fashion criminal, be a blot on the landscape.

社交ダンスが趣味だなんて、あんたの彼って意外にダサイのね。

Shakō-dansu ga shumi da nante, anta no kare tte igai ni dasai no ne.

I can't believe your boyfriend's into ballroom dancing. What a dweeb!

☞ Popularized in 1979, but in use before then on college campuses. Also *dasāi* and more vulgarly, *dasē*. The origin of the word is unclear, but it would be etymologically satisfying in the unlikely event that it derived from *dasaku* (駄作), "a crappy, crummy, second-rate piece of work (esp., artwork)."

dekkai (でっかい) "humongous" A Big, great big, monstrous, whopping.

この道路は狭いから、あんなでっかいリムジンじゃ通れないよ。

Kono dōro wa semai kara, anna dekkai rimujin ja tōrenai yo.

That guy'll never make it down this narrow street in that big ole limo.

☞ Stronger form of the colloquial *dekai* (huge), used primarily by men.

deretto (でれっと) "lax" Ad

1. Slovenly, sloppy, sluggardly.

パパは、休日は一日中でれっとしてテレビばかり観ている。

Papa wa, kyūjitsu wa ichinichi-jū deretto shite terebi bakari mite iru.

Dad really lets his hair down when he's got a day off. All he does is sit around in front of the TV.

2. Fawn over, drool over, make a fool of oneself in front of (a woman).

あんた、女の子の前にでると、すぐにでれっとなるのよね。

Anta, onna no ko no mae ni deru to, sugu ni deretto naru no yo ne.

Can't control yourself when you're around women, can you? You're lucky you don't step on your own tongue.

donpishari (どんぴしゃり) "slap-bang" A Right on, hit the mark, hit the bull's-eye, hit the nail on the head.

天気予報がどんぴしゃりとみごとに当たって、今日は晴天だね。

Tenki-yohō ga donpishari to migoto ni atatte, kyō wa seiten da ne.

Looks like the weather report was on the money today. It's a beautiful day.

☞ From *don*, an emphatic prefix, and *pishari*, onomatopoetic for a sharp slapping sound made by flat objects.

doronko (泥んこ) "muddy goo" N Mud. A Muddy.

道で転んで、新しいスーツが泥んこだらけになっちゃった。

Michi de koronde, atarashii sūtsu ga doronko darake ni natchatta.

My new suit got all covered with muck when I fell down in the road.

☞ A diminutive of *doro* (泥), the standard word for mud.

ero (エロ) N Erotica. A Erotic.

あいつはビニ本やエロビデオが好きで、エロな話しを平気でする。

Aitsu wa bini-bon ya ero-bideo ga suki de, ero na hanashi o heiki de suru.

The guy's into stuff like girlie mags and X-rated videos and doesn't think anything of telling dirty stories.

☞ Shortened from English "erotic."

gappori (がっぽり) "gouge" Ad (Make or lose money etc.) hand over fist, like nobody's business.

あの不動産屋のおやじは、土地の転売でがっぽり儲けてるのよ。

Ano fudōsan-ya no oyaji wa, tochi no tenbai de gappori mōkete 'ru no yo.

That real estate agent's making a killing (a bundle, a mint) turning over land.

gochagocha (ごちゃごちゃ) "hodgepodge" A Ad

1. All messed-up, all screwed-up.

この図書館は整理が悪くて本がごちゃごちゃにならんでる。

Kono tosho-kan wa seiri ga warukute hon ga gochagocha ni narande 'ru.

They're not very good at keeping things organized at this library. The books on the shelves are in a shambles.

2. Complaining, whining, whiny.

ごちゃごちゃ文句を言わずに、さっさと宿題をすませなさい。

Gochagocha monku o iwazu ni, sassa to shukudai o sumasenasai.

Quit moaning and groaning about everything and finish your homework.

☞ Synonymous, in its primary meaning, with *gotagota* and *goshagosha*.

gyūgyū (ぎゅうぎゅう) "squeezy" Ad

1. Packed (in) like sardines, all squished-up.

朝の通勤電車は、ぎゅうぎゅうに混んでいてすごく疲れてしまう。

Asa no tsūkin-densha wa, gyūgyū ni konde ite sugoku tsukarete shimau.

Riding those jampacked commuter trains in the morning really wears a guy out.

2. Be pressured, have the screws tightened on one.

課長にぼくの計算ミスがばれて、会社でぎゅうぎゅう絞られたよ。

Kachō ni boku no keisan-misu ga barete, kaisha de gyūgyū shiborareta yo.

They really came down hard on me (jumped down my throat) at the office when the section chief found out that I'd miscalculated some figures.

☞ Onomatopoetic for things rubbing together or being pressed together. Emphatic form of *kyūkyū*.

hachamecha (はちゃめちゃ) "whacko" Ⓐ Unsettled, mixed-up, all screwed-up, in havoc.

はちゃめちゃな性格のせいで、彼はアパートを追い出されたわ。

Hachamecha na seikaku no sei de, kare wa apāto o oidasareta wa.

He got kicked out of his apartment because he's so flakey.

真夜中に友達と飲んではちゃめちゃに騒いだので、警察が来ちゃった。

Ma-yonaka ni tomodachi to nonde hachamecha ni sawaida no de, keisatsu ga kichatta.

My friends and I were drinking and raising the roof in the middle of the night so the cops came.

☞ A variation on *mechamecha* (wacky), which is derived from *mechakucha* (mixed-up). Young people.

hentekorin (へんてこりん) "oddball" Ⓐ Funny-looking, weird, spacy.

彼はへんてこりんなデザインの食器ばかり集めるのが趣味なの。

Kare wa hentekorin na dezain no shokki bakari atsumeru no ga shumi na no.

He's into collecting these dishes with weird designs and stuff.

☞ *Henteko* (odd) plus *rin*, the latter lending a somewhat disparaging or humorous connotation, e.g., *chinchiku-rin* (dwarfy; skimpy), *chonchoko-rin* (lint, thingumabob), and *ponpoko-rin* (full [distended] tummy).

hitchaka-metchaka (ひっちゃかめっちゃか) "mishmash" Ⓐ In turmoil, pandemonium, a holy mess, an uproar.

ずっと掃除してないから、部屋の中はひっちゃかめっちゃかだ。

Zutto sōji shite 'nai kara, heya no naka wa hitchaka-metchaka da.

My room's a pigpen, I haven't straightened it up for ages.

国税局の強制監査で、社内はひっちゃかめっちゃかの状態です。

Kokuzei-kyoku no kyōsei-kansa de, shanai wa hitchaka-metchaka no jōtai desu.

What with the tax bureau auditing us and all, the office has been turned upside down.

☞ Like *hachamecha* and *mechamecha*, most likely from *mechakucha* (mixed-up).

hyonna (ひょんな) "baleful" Ⓐ Unexpected, surprise, strange.

昨日、ひょんな場所でひょんな人に会ったよ。だれだかわかる？

Kinō, hyonna basho de hyonna hito ni atta yo. Dare da ka wakaru?

You'll never guess who I bumped into the other day, or where, I'll bet.

まだ社内では秘密だけど、あの子とひょんな仲になっちゃった。

Mada shanai de wa himitsu da kedo, ano ko to hyonna naka ni natchatta.

Don't let on to anybody at the office that you know, but I've got this thing going with her.

hyorohyoro (ひょろひょろ) "tottery" A Ad

1. Unsteady on one's feet, to totter, stagger.

入院中の祖母は、ひょろひょろした足どりで歩いていたよ。

Nyūin-chū no sobo wa, hyorohyoro shita ashidori de aruite ita yo.

My grandma was wobbly on her feet when I saw her at the hospital.

2. [Of a person or flying object] weakly, barely.

そんなひょろひょろのボールを投げたら、すぐ打たれるぜ。

Sonna hyorohyoro no bōru o nagetara, sugu utareru ze.

You're gonna get blasted out of the pitcher's box if you throw bloopers (wimpy pitches) like that.

3. Tall and thin, gangling, spindly; [of a person] tall and lanky.

裏庭のひょろひょろのコスモスが、昨日の強い風で倒れたわ。

Ura-niwa no hyorohyoro no kosumosu ga, kinō no tsuyoi kaze de taoreta wa.

You know that tall, skinny cosmos in the back yard? Well, the strong wind yesterday blew it over.

ichikoro (いちころ) "one for a roll" Ad Curtains, it's all over.

この強力な殺虫剤を使えば、嫌なゴキブリもいちころで死ぬよ。

Kono kyōryoku na satchū-zai o tsukaeba, iya na gokiburi mo ichi-koro de shinu yo.

Use this industrial strength insecticide here and it's curtains for those pesky cockroaches.

あんな男、あたしがちょっと涙をみせれば簡単にいちころだわ。

Anna otoko, atashi ga chotto namida o misereba kantan ni ichikoro da wa.

With a guy like him, all I have to do is cry a little and he's a goner (and I have him wrapped around my little finger).

☞ From the notion that one blow *ichi(geki)* is enough to knock one down. *Koro* represents the sound of something rolling on the ground.

iisen iku (イイセンいく／いい線いく) "to go down a good line"

[Of an idea, approach, way of thinking, or relations between the sexes] be on the right track; [of a person's looks] not bad.

このアイディアはなかなかイイセンいってる。あと一息で正式な企画にできるよ。

Kono aidia wa nakanaka iisen itte 'ru. Ato hito-iki de seishiki na kikaku ni dekiru yo.

I think you're onto something with this idea. With a little more work, we can make it into a formal project.

森田君は男前だし、イイセンいってるから彼氏にしなさいよ。

Morita-kun wa otokomae da shi, iisen itte 'ru kara kareshi ni shi-nasai yo.

Morita's not bad looking, and things are going pretty well, so why don't you latch onto him?

ikeru (イケル) "can go" Ⓥ

1. [Of food or drink] be pretty good, taste good, be tasty.

この店の料理はなかなかイケルよ。特にソースがうまいね。

Kono mise no ryōri wa nakanaka ikeru yo. Toku ni sōsu ga umai ne.

The food here's not bad. The sauces are especially good.

2. Be a heavy drinker, be able to hold one's liquor.

君もけっこうイケル口だね？ さあ、どんどん飲もう飲もう。

Kimi mo kekkō ikeru kuchi da ne? Sā, dondon nomō nomō.

It looks like you can hold your own in the drinks department all right. Well, down the hatch.

ikkan no owari (一巻の終わり) "the reel's end" Ⓝ [Especially of life] curtains, the end of the line, all she wrote.

もしこの飛行機が墜落したら、乗員乗客全員が一巻の終わりだ。

Moshi kono hikō-ki ga tsuiraku shitara, jōin-jōkyaku zen'in ga ikkan no owari da.

If the plane goes down, that'll be all she wrote for everyone on board, passengers and crew alike.

☞ From its use by narrators of silent films announcing that the end had come; *ikkan* meaning one reel, or by extension a movie.

imaichi (いまいち) "one now" Ⓐⅾ Lack something, not be up to snuff, doesn't cut the mustard.

説明書を読んでも、このカメラの使い方がいまいちわからない。

Setsumei-sho o yonde mo, kono kamera no tsukaikata ga imaichi wa-karanai.

I still can't quite figure out how to work this camera even after reading the instruction book.

☞ A play on the second meaning of the standard *ima hitotsu* (今一つ; "one more [is needed]," "one [a little] short") by substituting *ichi* for *hitotsu*. Similar expressions include *ima-yon* and *ima-go*. Here *ima* is equivalent to *mō*. Used among young people.

imishin (意味深) "deep meaning" Ⓐ

1. More there than meets the eye, something there.

会長のことばは意味深だったな。辞任するつもりかも知れない。

Kaichō no kotoba wa imishin datta na. Jinin suru tsumori ka mo shi-renai.

There's more to what the chairman said than meets the eye. I'll bet
    he's planning to step down.
2. [Of the relationship between a man and woman] hot and heavy,
have something going, be getting it on.

ちょっと、あのふたりは意味深よ。何か秘密を隠してるみたいね。

*Chotto, ano futari wa imishin yo. Nani ka himitsu o kakushite 'ru mi-
tai ne.*

There's something going on between those two. They're trying to
    keep it secret, but I can tell.

☞ Shortened from *imi-shinchō* (意味深長; meaningful, significant). Originally
used by schoolgirls.

inchiki (いんちき) "cheat" Ⓐ

Bum, fake, fishy, phony, not what
it's cracked up to be, [of something said] a crock of shit.

通信販売で買った育毛剤はいんちきで、ちっとも効かなかった。

*Tsūshin-hanbai de katta ikumō-zai wa inchiki de, chitto mo kikana-
katta.*

The hair growth tonic I bought through a catalogue turned out to be a
    ripoff. It didn't do anything at all.

☞ Originally gambler's argot describing a fix, sting, or the perpetrator thereof.

ippashi (いっぱし) "one-edged" Ad

The real thing, the genuine
article.

研修生のくせに、いっぱしの営業マンみたいな態度の野郎だな。

*Kenshū-sei no kuse ni, ippashi no eigyō-man mitai na taido no yarō
da na.*

Who do you think you are, acting like you're a real salesman when
    you're nothing but a fucking trainee?

☞ Originally "once, one time." In the reading *ittan* (一端), the meaning is "in part,
partially."

kakko ii (カッコイイ) "good form" Ⓐ

Good-looking, righteous,
10, gnarly, bitchin, cherry, rad, wicked.

リチャード・ギアは、どんな役をしてもすてきでカッコイイわ。

Richādo Gia wa, donna yaku o shite mo suteki de kakko ii wa.

Doesn't matter what role he plays, Richard Gere is such a totally
    awesome stud (so studly).

サンダーバードは、ぼくのルノーより速いし、カッコイイ車だ。

Sandābādo wa, boku no Runō yori hayai shi, kakko ii kuruma da.

A Thunderbird's faster and sharper looking than my Renault.

☞ A corruption of *kakkō ga ii* (格好がいい).

kattarui (かったるい) "arm-dragging" Ⓐ

1. Beat, burned out, draggin' ass, pooped.

風邪で熱っぽいし、全身がかったるいから今日は会社を休もう。

Kaze de netsuppoi shi, zenshin ga kattarui kara kyō wa kaisha o yasumō.

I've got a cold and a fever and my whole body just feels so blah, I think I'll take the day off.

2. A hassle.

かったるいなあ。学校の便所掃除なんかまじめにしたかねえや。

Kattarui nā. Gakkō no benjo-sōji nanka majime ni shitakanē ya.

What a hassle, man. No way I can get into cleaning the toilets at school.

☞ A corruption of the old *kaina-darushi* (arm weary). *Kaina* (largely replaced by *ude*) is still used in sumo. *Darushi* is the modern *darui* (sluggish, listless).

kebai (けばい) **"glitzy"** Ⓐ [Especially of clothing, jewelry, or a person] flashy, gaudy, loud, trashy.

学生とは思えないケバイ女がこの女子大にはたくさんいるな。

Gakusei to wa omoenai kebai onna ga kono joshidai ni wa takusan iru na.

There's a bunch of girls going to this women's college that you'd never guess were students from the gaudy way they dress.

ココ・ピンクは、シャネルのなかでもかなりケバイ色の口紅よ。

Koko Pinku wa, Shaneru no naka de mo kanari kebai iro no kuchibeni yo.

Coco Pink is one of Chanel's louder lipsticks.

☞ From *kebakebashii* (glittery, gaudy). Used among young people.

kechon-kechon (けちょんけちょん) **"slap-bang"** Ⓐd Really (give someone hell, lay into someone), (chew someone's ass) up and down.

弟はバーでヤクザとけんかして、けちょんけちょんにやられた。

Otōto wa bā de yakuza to kenka shite, kechon-kechon ni yarareta.

My brother really caught hell from a bunch of yakuza in some bar.

ぼくの修士論文は、審査委員にけちょんけちょんにけなされた。

Boku no shūshi-ronbun wa, shinsa-iin ni kechon-kechon ni kenasareta.

The examiners really tore into (slammed, came down hard on) my master's thesis.

kinketsu (金欠) **"money deficient"** Ⓝ Broke, scraping the bottom of the barrel, cashed.

おれの月給は安いから、いくら倹約してもいつも金欠なんだ。

Ore no gekkyū wa yasui kara, ikura kenyaku shite mo itsumo kinketsu nan da.

My salary's so low that no matter how careful I am, I always end up broke by the end of the month.

☞ Shortened from *kinketsu-byō* (金欠病; financial anemia), a takeoff on *hinketsu-byō* (貧血病; anemia).

kinkirakin (きんきらきん) "sparkly" Ad Chichi, flashy, kitschy.

目立ちたいからって、髪までキンキラキンにする必要があるの？

Medachitai kara tte, kami made kinkirakin ni suru hitsuyō ga aru no?

I know you want to be different, but do you have to do that to your hair?

☞ For greater onomatopoetic effect, *kin* has been appended to the more standard *kinkira*, which has basically the same meaning.

kotteri (こってり) "thick" A

1. [Of food] rich, cloying; [of makeup] heavy, thick.

とんこつを使えば、とてもこってりした濃いスープがとれるわ。

Tonkotsu o tsukaeba, totemo kotteri shita koi sūpu ga toreru wa.

You can make some very rich, thick soup by using pork bones.

歌舞伎役者は、顔にこってりとお白粉をぬって舞台に立つのね。

Kabuki-yakusha wa, kao ni kotteri to oshiroi o nutte butai ni tatsu no ne.

Kabuki actors perform with thick white makeup on their faces.

2. [Of criticism] scathing, scorching, heavily.

試験でカンニングが見つかって、試験官にこってりしぼられた。

Shiken de kanningu ga mitsukatte, shiken-kan ni kotteri shiborareta.

The proctor really laid into me when he caught me cheating on the test.

kudoi (くどい) "drawn-out" A

1. Ad nauseam, (go) on and on.

年寄りの話し方はくどい。もっと簡潔にひと言でいえることなのに。

Toshiyori no hanashi-kata wa kudoi. Motto kanketsu ni hitokoto de ieru koto na no ni.

Why do old people have to go on and on about things they could just say in a couple words?

2. [Of tastes] too heavily seasoned, too heavy, too complex; [of colors or patterns] loud, gaudy, busy.

君のシチューは味付けがくどいよ。香辛料の入れすぎじゃないか。

Kimi no shichū wa ajitsuke ga kudoi yo. Kōshin-ryō no iresugi ja nai ka.

Your stews are just too heavy, like you've overseasoned them or something.

NATURE AND ALL THAT 119

☞ Probably derived from the standard *kudokudo*, which emphasizes boring repetitiousness by means of repetition.

kusai (臭い) "to stink" Ⓐ Funny, not right, shady, suspicious.

この横領事件では、どうもあの事務員が臭いから尾行してくれ。

Kono ōryō-jiken de wa, dōmo ano jimu-in ga kusai kara bikō shite kure.

As far as this embezzlement case is concerned, there's something fishy about that clerk. I want you to tail him.

あの交通事故は臭いぞ。事故に見せかけて殺したんじゃないか。

Ano kōtsū-jiko wa kusai zo. Jiko ni misekakete koroshita n' ja nai ka.

That traffic accident stinks to high heaven. He killed her and made it look like an accident, doncha think?

☞ Originally (and still) used about bad smells.

kusomiso (くそみそ) "shit and miso" Ⓐd Severely (criticize).

この小説はぼくの自信作なのに、編集者はくそみそに言うんだ。

Kono shōsetsu wa boku no jishin-saku na no ni, henshū-sha wa kuso-miso ni iu n' da.

I was really proud of the novel I wrote, but my editor thought it sucked (really ran it down).

☞ From the idea that things are so mucked-up that miso and shit can no longer be told apart. Also *misokuso*.

maji (まじ) "for serious" Ⓐ Seriously, for real, no shit.

3限は抜き打ち試験って、マジかよ。おれ、今日帰るからね。

San-gen wa nukiuchi-shiken tte, maji ka yo. Ore, kyō kaeru kara ne.

What, a pop quiz third period? You gotta be kiddin'. I'm splittin', man.

マジに告白するよ。おれと結婚してくれないか。おれは真剣だ。

Maji ni kokuhaku suru yo. Ore to kekkon shite kurenai ka. Ore wa shinken da.

No, really. I'm serious. Will you marry me?

☞ Shortened from *majime*, the standard word for "serious." *Maji* is most commonly found in interrogative sentences, and is used by young people.

mantan (満タン) "brimming tank" Ⓝ Fill 'er up, top it off.

レンタカーは、ガソリンを満タンにしてから返してくださいね。

Rentakā wa, gasorin o mantan ni shite kara kaeshite kudasai ne.

Please return the car with a full tank of gas.

☞ *Man* is "full" or "replete." *Tan* is short for *tanku*.

mechakucha (めちゃくちゃ) "mixed-up" Ⓐd Super, unbelievable, far out.

親戚のおばさんから、めちゃくちゃかわいい子猫をもらったの。

Shinseki no obasan kara, mechakucha kawaii ko-neko o moratta no.

I got this super cute little kitten from my aunt.

☞ Derived from *mecha*, which has the same primary meaning as *mechakucha* ("mixed-up," "disorderly," "illogical"), referring to both physical conditions and thought processes. *Kucha* adds onomatopoetic effect.

miemie (みえみえ) "seen-schmeen" Ⓐ Anybody can see, bare-faced, obvious, plain as the nose on one's face.

デートの帰りにホテルで休もうなんて、彼の下心はみえみえよ。

Dēto no kaeri ni hoteru de yasumō nante, kare no shitagokoro wa miemie yo.

It was as plain as day what he was up to, suggesting we check into a hotel to "rest up."

☞ A duplication of the noun *mie*, from the verb *mieru* (見える; to be visible).

mōchoi (もうちょい) "a bit more" Ⓐd A little more, one more push.

君はかわいいんだから、もうちょいやせればきっと男にモテる。

Kimi wa kawaii n' da kara, mōchoi yasereba kitto otoko ni moteru.

You're a cute chick. All you have to do is lose just a teeny bit more weight and you'll have to fight the guys off.

☞ Derived ultimately from the standard *mō chotto*. Mainly masculine usage.

moro ni (もろに) "all (at once)" Ⓐd Squarely, smack-dab, right.

あんな津波をもろに受けたら、このヨットは転覆してしまうよ。

Anna tsunami o moro ni uketara, kono yotto wa tenpuku shite shimau yo.

This yacht'd capsize for sure if a tidal wave like that smacked into it.

お酒を飲むと、森田のエッチな性格がもろに出て困るんだよな。

Osake o nomu to, Morita no etchi na seikaku ga moro ni dete komaru n' da yo na.

That Morita's such a horny bastard when he's got a few drinks in him that he becomes a real pest.

☞ From the prefix-like *moro* (諸), meaning "both of" or "all of (something)," as in *moro-te* (both hands) and *moro-bito* (all people). Sumo has *morozashi*.

motemote (モテモテ) "cart and carry" Ⓐ [Of a person] popular; [of a product] in, hot, red-hot.

健はハンサムだし背も高いから、女の子にモテモテの存在なの。

Ken wa hansamu da shi se mo takai kara, onna no ko ni motemote no sonzai na no.

Ken's good-looking and tall to boot. He has to beat the girls off with a stick.

布団乾燥機は、忙しい主婦にモテモテの大ヒット商品なんです。

Futon–kansō-ki wa, isogashii shufu ni motemote no daihitto shōhin nan desu.

Electric futon dryers are all the rage with busy housewives.

☞ Derived from the verb *moteru* (持てる; can carry, maintain, hold [people's attention]).

nānā (なあなあ) "Hey, what'd ya say" Ⓝ Back room politics; a nod and a wink; logrolling.

お米の市場開放は、なあなあではすまされない複雑な問題だね。

Okome no shijō-kaihō wa, nānā de wa sumasarenai fukuzatsu na mondai da ne.

Opening up the rice market is a problem that's too complicated to be worked out in back rooms with a nod and a wink.

この会議の運営委員はなあなあの仲で、きちんと審議をしない。

Kono kaigi no un'ei-iin wa nānā no naka de, kichin to shingi o shinai.

The members of the steering committee are so cheek by jowl with each other (so chummy) that nothing ever really gets properly discussed.

☞ From the use among male friends of the phrase *Nā, ii darō* ("Right?" or "What do you say?") when seeking agreement or support.

naui (ナウい) Ⓐ Hip, cool, in.

ファックスつきの留守番電話機が、いま一番ナウい電話なのよ。

Fakkusu-tsuki no rusuban–denwa-ki ga, ima ichiban naui denwa na no yo.

Answer phones that come complete with a fax and everything are the latest thing in telephones.

☞ From the English "now." Popular around 1980.

nechikkoi (ねちっこい) "gummy" Ⓐ Tenacious, persistent, be a badger.

あのボクサー、ねちっこいボディ攻撃が得意だよ。

Ano bokusā, nechikkoi bodi-kōgeki ga tokui da yo.

That boxer's known for the way he hammers away at the body.

☞ From the adverb *nechinechi* (sticky, persistent), with the adjective-forming *koi*, which indicates a superfluity.

ōboke (大ぼけ) "muddled in a big way" Ⓐ Doofus, out of it.

女の子と間違えてオカマに声かけるなんて、あいつも大ぼけだ。

Onna no ko to machigaete okama ni koe kakeru nante, aitsu mo ōboke da.

Guy's a real jewel. Imagine trying to pick up some fag thinking it was a chick!

☞ Among young people.

oishii (おいしい) **"tasty"** Ⓐ Cool, far out, good, sweet.

週2日働いて月収60万円なんておいしい仕事、あるわけない。

Shū-futsuka hataraite gesshū rokujū-man'en nante oishii shigoto, aru wake nai.

It's almost too good to be true, a job paying 600,000 yen a month for only two days work a week.

☞ Used among young people.

onboro (おんぼろ) **"good old rag"** ⒶⒹ Beat-up, run-down, on its last legs.

こんなおんぼろバスに乗るくらいなら、歩いたほうがましだわ。

Konna onboro-basu ni noru kurai nara, aruita hō ga mashi da wa.

I'd rather walk than ride a rattletrap bus like this.

☞ *On* is 御 ("honorable," or, here, the largely synonymous "good old"), and *boro* is a worn-out piece of cloth. Jocular.

on-no-ji (御の字) Ⓝ **"the character 'Honorable'"** Ⓝ Satisfying, gratifying, happier than pigs in clover (shit), more than one could ask for.

成績評価はＣだったけれど、単位がもらえただけでも御の字だ。

Seiseki-hyōka wa shī datta keredo, tan'i ga moraeta dake de mo on-no-ji da.

I just got a C, but I'm more than happy to take the units and run.

☞ From the idea that one feels so thankful for having achieved something that one would like to attach the character 御 ("honorable"; here pronounced *on*) to someone's or something's name in gratitude. Originally used in the Tokugawa-period red-light district.

ōppira (おおっぴら) **"wide open"** Ⓐ Openly, publicly, in front of everybody.

彼らのように人前でおおっぴらにキスするのには勇気がいるよ。

Karera no yō ni hitomae de ōppira ni kisu suru no ni wa yūki ga iru yo.

It takes a lot of guts to kiss right out in the open like they do.

☞ A corruption of the older *ōbira*, meaning "(the doors are) open wide (exposing the interior to public view)."

pechanko (ぺちゃんこ) **"squinched-up"** Ⓐ Flat(tened), squashed, frisbied.

地震で倒れた鉄骨に押しつぶされて、ぼくの車はぺちゃんこさ。

Jishin de taoreta tekkotsu ni oshitsubusarete, boku no kuruma wa pechanko sa.

Remember that earthquake we had the other day? Well, a steel beam fell on my car, and now it's as flat as a pancake.

☞ Derived from *pechan*, the sound or action of an inflated object being flattened, with the diminutive *ko*. Synonyms include the less emphatic *peshanko* and the more emphatic *petchanko*.

pekopeko (ぺこぺこ) "caved-in"

1. A Be dying of hunger, starving, so hungry one could eat a horse.

朝から何も食べずに仕事をしたから、あたしお腹がもうぺこぺこだわ。

Asa kara nani mo tabezu ni shigoto o shita kara, atashi onaka ga mō pekopeko da wa.

I've been working all morning without anything to eat, and I'm famished.

2. Ad Kowtow, fawn, toady, bootlick; brownnose, play up to, be a yes man.

山田は部長にぺこぺこ頭を下げるだけで、反論しないから信頼できないんだ。

Yamada wa buchō ni pekopeko atama o sageru dake de, hanron shinai kara shinrai dekinai n' da.

All Yamada ever does is kiss the department head's ass. He doesn't know what it means to have an opinion. Guy can't be trusted.

☞ From the original meaning of "dented," "depressed," or "caved-in" emerges the idea of the stomach being empty and sucked in, and the head, as it is bowed, being alternately extended and withdrawn.

pīchiku-pāchiku (ぴいちくぱあちく) "warbling" Ad [Of small children] chatter noisily, be chirpy.

子供は、どうしてあんなにピーチクパーチク騒々しいのかな。

Kodomo wa, dōshite anna ni pīchiku-pāchiku sōzōshii no ka na.

Sometimes I wonder what it is about little kids that makes 'em create such a racket.

☞ From the song of the lark.

pikkapika (ぴっかぴか) "glitter" Ad

1. Bright and shiny.

おかあさん、ぼくのエナメルの靴は、ピッカピカにみがいておいてくれよな。

Okāsan, boku no enameru no kutsu wa, pikkapika ni migaite oite kure yo na.

Hey, Mom, make sure you put a good shine on those patent leather shoes of mine, okay?

2. Brand (spanking) new.

兄貴は、買ったばかりのピッカピカの新車で事故ってしまった。

Aniki wa, katta bakari no pikkapika no shinsha de jikotte shimatta.

My big brother got in a fender-bender in his brand-new car.

☞ Emphatic form of *pikapika* (glitter, flicker, shine).

pinboke (ピンボケ) "unfocused" N Ad

1. [Of a photograph] out of focus, blurred.

メガネをしないで撮影したから、写真がみんなピンボケだった。

Megane o shinai de satsuei shita kara, shashin ga minna pinboke datta.

All the pictures are out of focus because I took them without my glasses on.

2. [Of a comment or opinion] miss the point, be off (wide of) the mark.

あたしの上司の助言はピンボケで、なんの助けにもならないわ。

Atashi no jōshi no jogen wa pinboke de, nan no tasuke ni mo naranai wa.

My boss is out there in left field. Nothing he says is of any help.
☞ *Pin* is the shortened form of *pinto*, from the Dutch word for focus, "brandpunt." *Boke* is from the verb *bokeru*, which means to be muddled or blurred.

pokkuri (ぽっくり) "snappily" Ad

1. [Of a tree, branch, or something similarly brittle] (break) with a snap, go "crack."

昨日の晩の台風で、庭の銀杏がポックリ折れてしまった。

Kinō no ban no taifū de, niwa no ichō ga pokkuri orete shimatta.

The typhoon the other night snapped the ginkgo tree in the yard right in two.

2. Die suddenly, drop dead, up and die one day.

あんなに元気だった祖父が、今朝急に脳出血でポックリ死んだ。

Anna ni genki datta sofu ga, kesa kyū ni nō-shukketsu de pokkuri shinda.

My grandpa was so chipper, and then he just up and died this morning from a cerebral hemorrhage.

pyokopyoko (ぴょこぴょこ) "hippity-hoppity" Ad

1. Hop.

ねえ、見て。カエルがピョコピョコはねて道路を横断してるわ。

Nē, mite. Kaeru ga pyokopyoko hanete dōro o ōdan shite 'ru wa.

Oh, look! A frog is hopping across the road.

2. Bob one's head.

ちっちゃなヒヨコがピョコピョコ餌を食べてるのはかわいいね。

Chitcha na hiyoko ga pyokopyoko esa o tabete 'ru no wa kawaii ne.

Isn't it cute the way those baby chicks peck away at the ground for food?
☞ A variation of *hyokohyoko*, which shares these two meanings.

rakuchin (楽ちん) "Mr. Easy" N A Easy, simple, easy as pie, have got it made, luck out.

ママが幼稚園まで車に乗せてってくれるから、ぼく楽ちんだよ。

Mama ga yōchi-en made kuruma ni nosete 'tte kureru kara, boku rakuchin da yo.

I'm really lucky 'cause Mommy takes me to kindergarten in the car.

☞ Used largely by children. *Raku* is "easy," and *chin* is a suffix indicating a person who has the attributes indicated by the preceding adjective or adverb: e.g., *debu-chin* (fatty + *chin* = fatso).

rakushō (楽勝) "easy win" N [Of a match or opponent] a pushover, cakewalk; [of something easy, such as a class at school] a snap, mick.

巨人軍にはいい投手がいるから、明日の試合も楽勝に違いない。

Kyojin-gun ni wa ii tōshu ga iru kara, ashita no shiai mo rakushō ni chigainai.

With the pitchers the Giants have got, tomorrow's game'll be a picnic.

rokusuppo (ろくすっぽ) "jeasly" Ad [Followed by a negative] half-assed, half-baked.

ろくすっぽ英語もできないくせに、アメリカ留学は不可能だよ。

Rokusuppo eigo mo dekinai kuse ni, Amerika-ryūgaku wa fu-kanō da yo.

There's no way you're gonna be able to study in the U.S. with your half-assed English.

☞ Jocular. The *roku* is likely the same as that in *roku-de-nashi* (worthless fellow) and *rokuroku* (hardly, [not] much). The derivation of *suppo* is unclear. Also *rokusuppō*.

saikō (サイコー／最高) "the highest" A Awesome, bitchin', far out, a ten, super, great, butt-kicking.

昨日のハマーは、サイコーだったわ。

Kinō no Hamā wa, saikō datta wa.

The Hammer concert last night was a blast.

☞ Since 1955. First used by college coeds, now common among young people.

saitē (サイテー／最低) "the lowest" A Fucked, piece of shit, suck, the pits.

きゃ、サイテー！さっきスーパーで買った牛乳腐ってるわ。

Kya, saitē! Sakki sūpā de katta gyūnyū kusatte 'ru wa.

What a bummer! The milk I just bought at the supermarket is sour!

☞ Since 1955. First used by college coeds; now among young people in general.

shiketa (しけた) "stormy" A Depressed, not popular, off.

ぼくが偶然入ったそのバーは、客もいなくてシケた店だったよ。

Boku ga gūzen haitta sono bā wa, kyaku mo inakute shiketa mise datta yo.

I went to some bar the other night that was really dead. There wasn't a soul in sight.

☞ Derived from the past tense of the verb *shikeru*, which originally referred to rough weather over the ocean.

shitsukoi (しつこい) "rich" Ⓐ

1. [Of tastes] unpleasantly greasy, heavy, spicy; [of colors] loud, clashing.

中華料理は油っこくて、しつこいからあんまり食べたくないわ。

Chūka-ryōri wa aburakkokute, shitsukoi kara anmari tabetaku nai wa.

I can't get into Chinese food 'cause it's so heavy and greasy.

2. Persistent, dogged, won't take no for an answer.

あんたってしつこいわ。嫌だって言ってるでしょ。鈍感な人ね！

Anta tte shitsukoi wa. Iya datte itte 'ru desho. Donkan na hito ne!

Leave me alone, will you! I told you I didn't like you. How dense can you get!

shotchū (しょっちゅう) "beginning and middle" Ad All the time, without letup, always.

あの二人は仲が悪くて、しょっちゅうけんかしてるんだ。

Ano futari wa naka ga warukute, shotchū kenka shite 'ru n' da.

Those two just can't seem to get along. They're at each other's throats night and day.

☞ Possibly a corruption of the older and little used *shochūgo* (初中後; the divisions of beginning, middle, and end; i.e., throughout).

soku (即) "to wit" Ad Right off, right away, on the spot.

電話で彼女にデートを申し込んだら、即ＯＫの返事をくれたよ。

Denwa de kanojo ni dēto o mōshikondara, soku ōkē no henji o kureta yo.

I called her up to ask her out, and she said yeah right then and there.

☞ The primary meaning is "namely, that is to say."

sugoi (すごい) "awesome" Ⓐ Real(ly), terribly; extremely, super.

クリスマス直前のデパートは、すごい混雑だから疲れちゃったわ。

Kurisumasu chokuzen no depāto wa, sugoi konzatsu da kara tsukarechatta wa.

The department store was super crowded (packed to the rafters) with Christmas shoppers. I'm really beat.

彼ね、あたしをすごい豪華なレストランに招待してくれたのよ。

Kare ne, atashi o sugoi gōka na resutoran ni shōtai shite kureta no yo.

He took me out to a deluxe restaurant that was out of this world.

☞ Used primarily among young people. *Suggoi* is more emphatic and *sugē* an even more emphatic and vulgar form used by men.

sukesuke (すけすけ) "doubly transparent" A See-through, sheer.

あの女、すけすけのブラウス着てるから下着がまる見えだぜ。

Ano onna, sukesuke no burausu kite 'ru kara shitagi ga marumie da ze.

Check out that chick! Her blouse is so thin you can see her bra right through it.

☞ From the verb *sukeru* (透ける; to be transparent).

sukkarakan (すっからかん) "taken aback" A Completely empty; broke, flat broke.

バイトで稼いだ金をパチンコですって、ぼくはすっからかんだ。

Baito de kaseida kane o pachinko de sutte, boku wa sukkarakan da.

I blew all the bread I made at my part-time job playing pachinko, so I'm tapped out.

☞ Portmanteau from *sukkari* (all) and *akkerakan* (jolted, dumbfounded).

supponpon (すっぽんぽん) "bare tummy" A Naked, stark naked, in one's birthday suit, naked as a jaybird.

お父さん、すっぽんぽんで部屋の中を歩くのはやめてください。

Otōsan, supponpon de heya no naka o aruku no wa yamete kudasai.

Hey Dad, give me a break and stop walkin' around the house stark naked, will ya!

☞ Probably from *su* (indicating an extreme condition) and *ponpon* (tom-tom; baby talk for stomach, coming from the sound of the tummy being playfully patted or thumped). A more standard synonym is *suppadaka* (*su* + *hadaka*).

suttamonda (すったもんだ) "rubbing and kneading" Ad Wrangle, row, fracas, falling-out.

父の遺産相続ですったもんだの末、結局は裁判ざたになったわ。

Chichi no isan-sōzoku de suttamonda no sue, kekkyoku wa saiban-zata ni natta wa.

There was such a big fuss over who was going to get what from my dad's estate that we ended up going to court.

☞ From the verbs *suru* (to rub) and *momu* (to knead or massage), suggesting that, in order to resolve a dispute, someone is rubbing the backs and massaging the shoulders of the disputants.

sutten-kororin (すってんころりん) "slippin' and fallin'" Ad

Trip and fall, fall flat on one's face.

凍った道路ですってんころりんと転んで、右腕折っちゃったよ。

Kōtta dōro de sutten-kororin to koronde, migi-ude otchatta yo.

I went and broke my right arm when I slipped and fell on an icy
road.

☞ Probably from *sutten* (an emphatic corruption of *suten*, the sound of an object
or person falling or slipping with considerable force) and *korori* (the sound of a
small object dropping or a person falling or flopping down). Also *sutten-korori*,
which is considered more standard.

suttonkyō (すっとんきょう) "absolutely bizarre" Ⓐ [Of speech
or behavior] wild, weird, freaky.

あいつが、急にすっとんきょうな声を出すからみんな驚いたよ。

Aitsu ga, kyū ni suttonkyō na koe o dasu kara minna odoroita yo.

He scared the hell out of everybody when all at once he lets out with
this unearthly screech.

☞ Emphatic form of *tonkyō* (頓狂), with the prefix *su* indicating an extremity.

tarafuku (たらふく) "cod belly" Ⓐd Be full, stuffed (to the gills),
ready to burst; eat one's fill, pig out, pork out.

今日はおれがおごるよ。みんな、たらふく食っていいぞ。

Kyō wa ore ga ogoru yo. Minna, tarafuku kutte ii zo.

Everything's on me today, so you all just pitch in and eat your fill.

☞ Often written 鱈腹 (codfish belly), this is an homophonic equivalent. The origin of the word is unclear.

tenurui (手ぬるい) "hand-lax" Ⓐ Half-hearted, lax, not tough.

警察の駐車違反取り締まりが手ぬるいから、道路は渋滞しっぱなしだ。

*Keisatsu no chūsha-ihan–torishimari ga tenurui kara, dōro wa jūtai
shippanashi da.*

There are traffic jams everywhere you go because the cops don't
crack down on parking violations.

☞ *Nurui* (modern "lukewarm") here retains an older meaning (lax, loose, lenient),
equivalent to contemporary *yurui* (緩い).

tenya-wanya (てんやわんや) "every man for himself" Ⓐd
1. Go crazy, go wild, be in pandemonium.

地元の野球チームが優勝したんで、町中てんやわんやの大騒ぎさ。

*Jimoto no yakyū-chīmu ga yūshō shita n' de, machi-jū tenya-wanya
no ōsawagi sa.*

The whole town's going crazy because the local baseball team won
the championship.

2. Be jumbled-up, in a state of confusion.

昨日は家の引っ越しでね、家中てんやわんやの大忙しだったの。

*Kinō wa ie no hikkoshi de ne, uchi-jū tenya-wanya no ōisogashi
datta no.*

There was a big to-do at my house yesterday, what with moving and all.
☞ Said to be a corrupted combination of *tenden* ("hand in hand") and *waya* (reckless, unreasonable).

tobikiri (とびきり) "jump and slash" Ad Incredibly, indescribably; super, outa sight.

とびきり上等な牛肉を買ったら、やっぱりとてもおいしいわね。

Tobikiri jōtō na gyūniku o kattara, yappari totemo oishii wa ne.

I bought this out-of-sight cut of quality beef, and you know, it's true, it was really delicious.
☞ From 飛び切り (jump high in the air and slash one's opponent)—a swordfighting technique. Also, more emphatically, *tobikkiri*.

tokkae-hikkae (とっかえひっかえ) "swap and trade" Ad First one and then another, one after another.

新しいセーターをとっかえひっかえ試着したけれど、買わなかったわ。

Atarashii sētā o tokkae-hikkae shichaku shita keredo, kawanakatta wa.

I kept trying on one sweater after another, but ended up not buying anything.
☞ Corruption of *torikae-hikikae* (取り替え引き替え) with the same meaning.

tokku no mukashi ni (とっくのむかしに) "way back when" Ad Ages ago, long ago, way back.

『二都物語』なら、とっくの昔に読んだよ。ディケンズのだろ？

"Nito-monogatari" nara, tokku no mukashi ni yonda yo. Dikenzu no daro?

A *Tale of Two Cities*? Yeah, I read that way back when. Dickens, right?
☞ Corruption of *toku* (adverbial form of *toshi*), in the sense of "earlier," the remainder of the phrase being standard. Likewise *toku ni* has become *tokku ni* (long ago, ages ago).

tonchinkan (とんちんかん) "ge-bang ge-bong" A Off base, off the wall, wacky.

人の話をよく聞いていないから、吉田さんはとんちんかんな質問ばかりりする。

Hito no hanashi o yoku kiite inai kara, Yoshida-san wa tonchinkan na shitsumon bakari suru.

That Yoshida's always asking these off-the-wall questions 'cause he never listens to what anybody's sayin'.
☞ From the sound of the blacksmith's hammer followed by that of his helper as they strike an anvil slightly out of sync.

tsuite 'ru (ついてる) "it's with me" V Luck out, have all the luck, be on a roll, today's one's day.

あんな美人とデートできるなんて、おまえついてるじゃないか。

Anna bijin to dēto dekiru nante, omae tsuite 'ru ja nai ka.

You're one lucky sucker to be going out with a 10 like her.

☞ Shortened from *tsuite iru* (to have [good luck] adhere to oneself), from *tsuku*, "to stick to."

tsūkā (つうかあ) "Right? Right on" N Know each other inside out, be just like that.

おれたち二人はツーカーだから、何も言わなくてもわかるのさ。

Ore-tachi futari wa tsūkā da kara, nani mo iwanakute mo wakaru no sa.

We're on the same wavelength, so we don't really have to say anything to understand each other.

☞ From the expression, *Tsū to ieba kā* (if one says *tsū*, the other says *kā*). The exact meaning of *tsū* and *kā* is unclear.

tsuntsuruten (つんつるてん) "slickarooney" A Too short; [of pants] high-water, where's the flood.

ウールのセーターを洗濯したら、縮んでつんつるてんになった。

Ūru no sētā o sentaku shitara, chijinde tsuntsuruten ni natta.

My wool sweater shrunk right up when I washed it.

☞ The formation of this word is unclear, but the original meaning focuses on the bared legs revealed by an overly short kimono.

urusai (うるさい) "noisy" A Discriminating, fussy, particular, picky.

パパは料理の味にうるさいから、ママは毎日苦労しているのよ。

Papa wa ryōri no aji ni urusai kara, mama wa mainichi kurō shite iru no yo.

My dad's really finicky about what he eats, so my mom's got her work cut out for her deciding what to cook.

wansa (わんさ) "gaggling" Ad In droves, swarms, throngs.

君の会社が新入社員を募集したら、わんさと応募があるだろう。

Kimi no kaisha ga shinnyū-shain o boshū shitara, wansa to ōbo ga aru darō.

I'll bet if you guys advertised for help, you'd be flooded with applicants.

☞ Originally, a large number of people (a gaggle) thronging noisily together.

warikashi (わりかし) "dividing-up" Ad Relatively, pretty.

田原屋のカツレツは、わりかし大きくて昔から人気があるんだ。

Tawara-ya no katsuretsu wa, warikashi ōkikute mukashi kara ninki ga aru n' da.

The pork cutlets at Tawara-ya come in fair-sized portions and have been popular as far back as I can remember.

☞ A corruption of *warikata* (割方; Dutch treat, relatively). Used by young people.

yabai (やばい) "chancy" Ⓐ Be in for it, catch it.

あの先公にタバコ吸ってるの見られたら、やばいことになるぜ。

Ano senkō ni tabako sutte 'ru no miraretara, yabai koto ni naru ze.

Shit's gonna hit the fan (You're gonna be in for it) if that teacher sees you smokin'.

☞ Originally used by criminals, *yabai* is now part of the youth culture, especially male. Also, and more vulgarly, *yabē*, used by young men.

yattoko (やっとこ) "at long last" Ⓐd Finally, at last.

あの人の家をやっとこ見つけたら、もう引っ越したあとだった。

Ano hito no ie o yattoko mitsuketara, mō hikkoshita ato datta.

By the time I tracked him down, he'd already pulled up stakes.

☞ Derived from *yatto* (at last, finally, barely).

yoppodo (よっぽど) "a goodly degree" Ⓐd Much, way; have a good mind to.

あなたのほうが、あいつよりもよっぽどハンサムでカッコイイ。

Anata no hō ga, aitsu yori mo yoppodo hansamu de kakko ii.

You're way better lookin' than he is and a whole lot sharper dresser, too.

上司にうるさく注意されて、よっぽど殴ってやろうかと思った。

Jōshi ni urusaku chūi sarete, yoppodo nagutte yarō ka to omotta.

The way my boss was riding me, I was just this far from letting him have it.

☞ More emphatic than *yohodo*.

zakkubaran (ざっくばらん) Ⓐ Straightforward, up front, open, frank.

ざっくばらんに言おう。君はこの会社に必要のない人間なんだ。

Zakkubaran ni iō. Kimi wa kono kaisha ni hitsuyō no nai ningen nan da.

I'll make no bones about it. We can get along well enough here at the office without you.

彼はざっくばらんで、とても自分に正直な人だから尊敬できる。

Kare wa zakkubaran de, totemo jibun ni shōjiki na hito da kara sonkei dekiru.

He's a straight-shooter, completely honest with himself. You have to respect the guy.

zukezuke (ずけずけ) "straight off" Ⓐd Bluntly, without mincing

one's words, call a spade a spade.

他人にずけずけとものを言うようなやつは、バカに決まっている。

Ta'nin ni zukezuke to mono o iu yō na yatsu wa, baka ni kimatte iru.

Anybody that's as outspoken about things as that's gotta be stupid.

Interjections and Exclamations:
Aargh, Truthfully, and Gong

abayo (あばよ) **"if that's it"** Later, See ya, So long, Catch (see) you later.

おれは、あてのない旅にでることにしたぜ。あばよ。元気でな。

Ore wa, ate no nai tabi ni deru koto ni shita ze. Abayo. Genki de na.

Catch you later, man. I'm hitting the road just to see where I end up. Take care.

☞ Possibly shortened from *sāraba yo* or *saraba yo*, an older version of the modern *sō de areba* with the emphatic particle *yo* appended. Much more colloquial and emotionally nuanced than *sayonara*. Used among close male friends.

akanbē (あかんべえ) **"red eye"** Ⓝ A gesture of disdain or rejection made to someone or behind someone's back (like thumbing one's nose), in which the bottom eyelid is pulled down, exposing the inner veined surface; an exclamation accompanying such a gesture: [children] "na-na-nana-na," "go fly a kite," "go jump in the lake"; [adults] "my eye," "drop dead," "go to hell," "go to the devil," "stuff it."

あかんべえ！死んだってあんたの手伝いなんかするもんか。

Akanbē! Shinda tte anta no tetsudai nanka suru mon ka.

Don't make me laugh! I'd rather die an awful death than help you out.

☞ Corruption of *akame* (red eye). Also *akanbe* and *akkanbē*. Used most often by women and children.

bārō (バァロー) **"schmuck"** Ass, fool, numbnuts, shit-for-brains.

バァロー。おれの大切なコニャック、おまえ全部飲んだだろう？

Bārō. Ore no taisetsu na konyakku, omae zenbu nonda darō?

Hey, asshole! What'd you go and do, drink all my cognac?

☞ The first and last syllables of *baka yarō*. Used by young people.

betsunī (別にー) **"(not) especially"** Doesn't matter (to me); nothing, nothing special, not much.

そろそろお昼ね。ねえ、お昼御飯に、あんた何食べたい？／何って聞かれても、別にー。ぼくはまだお腹すいてないもの。

Sorosoro ohiru ne. Nē, ohiru-gohan ni, anta nani tabetai? / Nani tte kikarete mo, betsunī. Boku wa mada onaka suite 'nai mono.

It's almost time for lunch. Whadaya feel like eating? / Nothing, really, now that you ask. I'm not very hungry yet.
☞ Used by young people since 1983. Pronunciation drawn out at the end.

bū (ぶう) "gong" [Used in response to an oral comment to indicate somewhat jocularly that the comment is off base] Wrong! Guess again!

あんたの彼氏、日に焼けてるわね。サーフィンするんでしょ？／ブー！あいつは泳げないの。日焼けサロンに通ってるだけよ。

Anta no kareshi, hi ni yakete 'ru wa ne. Sāfin suru n' desho? / Bū! Aitsu wa oyogenai no. Hiyake-saron ni kayotte 'ru dake yo.

Your boyfriend's really got a boss tan! He's a surfer, right? / Wrong! He can't even swim. That's from going to one of those tanning salons.
☞ Said to come from the sound of the buzzer signifying an incorrect answer on a quiz show. Another less plausible theory holds that it derives from the English "Boo!" Used by young people among peers.

chanchan (ちゃんちゃん) "clappity-clap" That's all she wrote; period.

歴史の期末試験、全然解答できなくてチャンチャン。留年だわ。

Rekishi no kimatsu-shiken, zenzen kaitō dekinakute chanchan. Ryūnen da wa.

I like really bombed on the history final. But, hey, that's the way it goes. Have to take it again next year, I guess.
☞ Used by young people to indicate the end of a comment about something inconsequential or boring. Possibly from *shanshan*, a rhythmic and ritualistic clapping of the hands to mark the settlement of some affair or conclusion of an event. Extremely colloquial.

che' (ちぇっ) "sheesh" Crud, damn, fuck, God, shit, shee-it.

ちぇっ、失敗した。このカンフー映画、全然おもしろくないや。

Che', shippai shita. Kono kanfū-eiga, zenzen omoshiroku nai ya.

Shit, man. I really blew it. This kung-fu flick really sucks.
☞ Origin unclear. Used primarily by men. Also *che*.

chichinpuipui (ちちんぷいぷい) "hocus-pocus" [Used as an incantation of sorts to introduce a bit of supposed magic or legerdemain; sometimes said when rubbing a child's injury to soothe the pain] abracadabra, voila; kiss it and make it go away.

もう泣かないでね。チチンプイプイ、痛いの痛いの飛んでけー。

Mō nakanaide ne. Chichinpuipui, itai no itai no tonde 'kē.

Don't cry now, okay. Mommy'll kiss it and make it better.

chikushō (ちくしょう) "birds and beasts" Damn, damn it.

ちくしょう、今月の販売成績でまたあいつに抜かれてしまった。

Chikushō, kongetsu no hanbai-seiseki de mata aitsu ni nukarete shi-matta.

Damn if he didn't outsell me this month again.

☞ Originally a Buddhist term (畜生) for beasts—animals, birds, fish and insects—viewed as reincarnations of those whose karma from previous existences warranted demotion.

chiwa (ちわ) "howdy" Hi, hi ya, hey, hey there, what's up, afternoon.

チワ、先輩！放課後はどんなトレーニングから始めましょうか。

Chiwa, senpai! Hōka-go wa donna torēningu kara hajimemashō ka.

Afternoon! What exercises do you want us to start with after school?

☞ Shortened form of *konnichiwa*. Extremely colloquial greeting used by men, students, or merchants making home visits to take orders. Not used among family members or close friends.

chīzu (チーズ) (Say) cheese, smile at the birdie.

写真を撮りますから、ちゃんとレンズを見てね。はい、チーズ。

Shashin o torimasu kara, chanto renzu o mite ne. Hai, chīzu.

I'm ready to take the picture, so everyone look at the camera. Okay. Say "cheese."

choito (ちょいと) "(wait) a bit" Hey there, you there, whoa.

ちょいと、酒屋さん。あとでお醤油を１本届けてくれるかしら。

Choito, sakaya-san. Ato de oshōyu o ippon todokete kureru kashira.

Yoo-hoo! Could I get you to deliver a bottle of soy sauce later?

☞ Friendly way to get someone's attention. Used by older women.

don-mai (ドンマイ) Don't let it get to you, don't sweat it, it's cool, no big deal, shake it off.

ドンマイ、ドンマイ。次のセットは必ずおれたちがとるんだぞ。

Don-mai, don-mai. Tsugi no setto wa kanarazu ore-tachi ga toru n' da zo.

It's alright, it's alright. We'll get 'em next set for sure.

☞ From the English "don't mind."

ettō (えっとう) "ya know" Like, uh, er, well.

エットー、それは、エットー、どういう言い訳すればいいのか...。

Ettō, sore wa, ettō, dō iu iiwake sureba ii no ka....

Uh, that's uh, gee, I'm kinda at a loss to explain ...

☞ Used primarily by young people. The standard expression is *ēto*.

ganbaranakutcha (がんばらなくっちゃ) "(we must) stick in there" (We've gotta) hang in there, tough it out, suck it up.

期末試験まであとたった2日しかないわ。がんばらなくっちゃ。

Kimatsu-shiken made ato tatta futsuka shika nai wa. Ganbarana-kutcha.

Just two more days till mid-terms. Gotta really reach down deep.

☞ Shortened from *ganbaranakereba naranai.*

gē (げえ) "aargh" Barf, yuck.

ゲー、またカレーかい。これで3日連続だよ。もううんざりだ。

Gē, mata karē kai. Kore de mikka-renzoku da yo. Mō unzari da.

Not curry again! Jeez, I think I'm gonna barf. That makes three days in a row. I've had it up to here.

☞ Used by children and young people. Vulgar.

gochisōsama (ごちそうさま) "what a treat" [Jocularly after listening to someone talk glowingly about a sexual partner or seeing a couple making out] Gee, thanks; That was fun.

彼みたいに男らしくて頼れる人は他に考えられないのよね。／まあ、ごちそうさま。あんたは一生ずっとのろけてなさいよ。

Kare mitai ni otoko rashikute tayoreru hito wa hoka ni kangaerarenai no yo ne. / Mā, gochisōsama. Anta wa isshō zutto norokete 'nasai yo.

I can't imagine anybody more reliable or studly than my boyfriend. / Gee, thanks, that's just what I wanted to hear. You go right ahead and spend your whole life doting over him.

hontō (ホントー) "truthfully" No kidding? Wow! Oh, yeah? You don't say?

会社の帰りにデパートで買い物してきちゃった。／ホントー。

Kaisha no kaeri ni depāto de kaimono shite kichatta. / Hontō.

I dropped by a department store on my way home from work. / Oh, really?

☞ Also *honto.* Used by young people.

hyūhyū (ひゅうひゅう) "wowee" [Jocularly, at the sight of a couple making out] get it on, hot stuff, hubba-hubba.

噂のカップル、幸治と花子のお出ましだわ。／ヒューヒュー！

Uwasa no kappuru, Kōji to Hanako no odemashi da wa. / Hyūhyū!

Here come the happy couple now, Kōji and Hanako. / Hubba-hubba.

☞ From the sound of a wolf whistle.

iida (イーだ) "fine (with me)" Humph, who cares, okay for you.

イーだ！浩ってサイテーの男ね。謝ったって絶対に許さない！

Iida! Hiroshi tte saitē no otoko ne. Ayamatta tte zettai ni yurusanai!

Humph! You're such an asshole, Hiroshi! I don't care if you do apol-

ogize, I'm never forgiving you.
☞ Emphatic for *ii*, used by women and children to or about someone who has just expressed dislike of or unwillingness to do something. Also *ii'da* (イイッだ).

ikki-ikki (イッキイッキ) "one breath, one breath" Chug-a-lug, go man go.

まず一杯は、一息で飲みほすんだぞ。それっ、イッキ！イッキ！
Mazu ippai wa, hito-iki de nomihosu n' da zo. Sore', ikki! Ikki!
You've gotta down this sucker first. Chug it, man. Chug it!
☞ At drinking parties to encourage someone (egg them on) to drain a glass or bottle, usually of beer, without lowering it from their mouth.

iyō (いよう) "and a one … " [Said when praising, teasing, or starting something like the communal clapping done to a 3-3-7 rhythm that so often ends a party in Japan].

イヨー、久しぶり。おまえにはもう10年会ってなかったな。
Iyō, hisashiburi. Omae ni wa mō jū-nen atte 'nakatta na.
Hey! Long time, no see. Must be ten years, huh?

イヨー、ご両人、あいかわらず円満な夫婦生活を演じてますね。
Iyō, goryōnin, aikawarazu enman na fūfu-seikatsu o enjite 'masu ne.
Far out! You two look like married life's still agreeing with you.

それでは皆様、お手を拝借。イヨー。(三三七拍子)
Sore de wa minasama, ote o haishaku. Iyō. (Sansannana-byōshi)
Okay everybody, ready? Here we go! [clapping to 3-3-7 rhythm]
☞ Used by men. Also *iyo, yō* and *yo*.

jā (じゃあ) "if that's it"
1. So, well.

8時までに帰宅しないと、ワイフがうるさいので。じゃあ、さよなら。
Hachi-ji made ni kitaku shinai to, waifu ga urusai no de. Jā, sayonara.
The old lady throws a fit if I'm not home by eight, so I guess I'd better be going.
2. In that case, then.

今夜は先約があるんで、悪いけどそっちには行けないんだ。／じゃあ、また機会があったらぜひいっしょに飲んで騒ごうね。
Kon'ya wa senyaku ga aru n' de, warui kedo sotchi ni wa ikenai n' da. / Jā, mata kikai ga attara zehi issho ni nonde sawagō ne.
Sorry, but I've got something planned for tonight, so I won't be able to make it over. / Well, let's get together and party some other time then, huh?
☞ Corruption of *de wa.* Used among close friends. See also *jāne.*

jajajajān (じゃじゃじゃじゃあん) "ta-ta-ta-tat-ta-ta"

ジャジャジャジャーン！発表します。ぼくついに婚約しました。

Jajajajān! Happyō shimasu. Boku tsui ni konyaku shimashita.

Can I have a drum roll, please. I have an important announcement to make. Yours truly is now engaged to be married.

☞ Used by young people to introduce—somewhat pompously—an important announcement or when seeing or hearing something of import. From the first four notes of Beethoven's Symphony No. 5 in C minor.

jāne (じゃあね) "if that's it, then" Catch ya later; I'm outa here; later; see ya (around).

今夜は彼とお食事するのよ。もう出かけなくちゃ。じゃあね。

Kon'ya wa kare to oshokuji suru no yo. Mō dekakenakucha. Jāne.

I'm havin' dinner with my boyfriend tonight, so I've gotta run. See you guys later.

☞ Corruption of *de wa* plus sentence-ending *ne*. Not appropriate for addressing one's superiors. See also *jā*.

kamone (かもね) "could be" Good chance, maybe, yeah, who knows.

あいつ、彼女にふられたのがショックで、自殺しちゃうかもね。

Aitsu, kanojo ni furareta no ga shokku de, jisatsu shichau kamone.

He's taking getting dumped by his girlfriend pretty hard. You know, he could just go off and kill himself.

ぼくの会社も、不景気の影響で倒産するのかなあ。／かもね。

Boku no kaisha mo, fu-keiki no eikyō de tōsan suru no ka nā. / Kamone.

I can't help but wonder if the place I work is gonna belly up with this recession and all. / Just might.

☞ Used primarily by women, *kamone* is formed by joining *ka mo* from *ka mo shirenai*, and *ne*, the sentence-ending particle used to seek or express agreement. Very colloquial. Not appropriate when addressing superiors. Also *kamoyo*, slightly stronger than *kamone*.

kono yarō (この野郎) "this field man" Bastard, fucker, motherfucker.

この野郎、黙ってりゃいい気になりやがって。とんでもないやつだ！

Kono yarō, damatte 'rya ii ki ni nariyagatte. Tonde mo nai yatsu da!

You're one dumb motherfucker! Give ya an inch and ya take a mile.

なんだ、この野郎！文句があるなら、オレにハッキリ言えばいいだろう！

Nan da, kono yarō! Monku ga aru nara, ore ni hakkiri ieba ii darō!

Hey, fucker! What's yer problem? Spit it out.

☞ *Yarō* has had a number of meanings (including male prostitute), of which one, as indicated by the kanji, was country bumpkin.

kuso (くそ) **"shit"** Shit, shi', shee-it.

クソ！兄貴のやつ、おれの車をまた無断で乗っていっちゃった。

Kuso! Aniki no yatsu, ore no kuruma o mata mudan de notte itchatta.

Shit! That asshole brother of mine went and took my car again without asking.

☞ Used primarily by men. Also *kuso'*.

makesō (負けそう) **"looks like (I'm) going to lose"** Can't keep up with, be out of one's league.

小学生のうちから夜遊びが大好きだなんて、もう負けそうだわ。

Shōgaku-sei no uchi kara yoasobi ga daisuki da nante, mō makesō da wa.

A party animal when she was still in grammar school! No way I can keep up!

一度にビッグ・マックを10個も食べられるなんて、負けそう。

Ichido ni biggu-makku o jukko mo taberareru nante, makesō.

Guy's unreal, scarfin' 10 Big Macs in one sitting! Outa my league, man!

☞ Used by young people.

māmā (まあまあ) **"there, there"**
1. Come on; easy does it; now, now; there now; come, come.

まあまあ、そんなにカッカしないで、少し落ち着いてください。

Māmā, sonna ni kakka shinai de, sukoshi ochitsuite kudasai.

Easy there, big guy. Don't ge'cher balls in an uproar. Chill out.
2. [Used by women] goodness gracious, good heavens.

まあまあ、こんな遠いところまで、よくおいでくださいました。

Māmā, konna tōi tokoro made, yoku oide kudasaimashita.

My goodness! What a pleasure it is to see you out this way! / Well, I'll be! What brings you out to this neck of the woods?

matane (またね) **"again, then"** Catch you later; later; let's get together again sometime; see you around.

今夜は楽しかった。でももう帰らなければならないの。またね。

Kon'ya wa tanoshikatta. Demo mō kaeranakereba naranai no. Matane.

I really had a good time tonight, but I think it's time for me to be going. I'll see you later.

☞ Not used when addressing superiors. Used primarily by women.

nanchatte (なんちゃって) **"what (am I) saying"** I wish, You wish, Not.

これから美女とふたり、ホテルで朝までエッチ、なんちゃって。

Kore kara bijo to futari, hoteru de asa made etchi, nanchatte.

After this I'm gonna meet this stone fox at a hotel and do the wild thing till morning. Not!

☞ From *nan to itte* (何と言って). Since 1978, when rumors of an imaginary character by the name of Nanchatte Ojisan (Uncle Nanchatte) were popular. Used by young people. Also *nānchatte*.

ottotto (おっとっと) **"oops oops"** Oops, whoops [uttered upon almost losing one's balance, stumbling, dropping, running into, or spilling something].

おっとっと。高層ビルの屋上から下を見てるとめまいがするよ。

Ottotto. Kōsō-biru no okujō kara shita o mite 'ru to memai ga suru yo.

Steady now, big guy. Looking down from the top of one of these tall buildings really makes me dizzy.

おっとっと、あぶないなあ。ちゃんと前をみて運転してくれよ。

Ottotto, abunai nā. Chanto mae o mite unten shite kure yo.

Whew! That was a close call. Keep your eyes on the road, will you!

おっとっと、ありがとう。じゃ、みんなで乾杯といきますか。

Ottotto, arigatō. Ja, minna de kanpai to ikimasu ka.

That's enough, that's enough! Thanks. Well, what do you guys say we have a little toast?

☞ Derived from *otto*, which has basically the same meaning along with a number of others. Also *ottottotto*.

pinpon (ピンポン) **"ding-dong"** Right; that's right; yes, you've got it.

家の前においてある黒いポルシェは君の車かい？／ピンポン！

Ie no mae ni oite aru kuroi Porushe wa kimi no kuruma kai? / Pinpon!

Is that black Porsche out in front of the house yours? / Sure is!

☞ From the sound of a quiz-show bell ringing to indicate a correct response. Used by young people among peers.

pīsu (ピース) Peace [used ubiquitously by children and young people when posing for a picture or indicating that things are going well. Word is usually repeated and accompanied by the "V" sign. It has nothing to do with the notion of "peace"].

一次の面接はどうだったの？／ピース、ピース。楽勝だった。

Ichiji no mensetsu wa dō datta no? / Pīsu, pīsu. Rakushō datta.

So, how did the first interview go? / Smooth as silk. I aced it.

☞ Since 1971.

shimeshime (しめしめ) **"it's all mine"** I'm in luck, Today's my day, Yes.

しめしめ。試験監督が席を離れたぞ。カンニングするなら今だ。

Shimeshime. Shiken-kantoku ga seki o hanareta zo. Kanningu suru nara ima da.

Alright! The proctor's out of the room. Gonna cheat, now's the time.

☞ Shortened from *shimeta-shimeta*, which carries the same meaning. Ultimately from the verb *shimeru* (占める; to mark off territory as one's own). Spoken under one's breath or to oneself when one is pleased that things seem to be going one's way.

shīn (シーン) **"a hush"** I don't hear any applause; You wish.

社内で一番カッコイイのは、やっぱりぼくですよね。二枚目だしね。／シーン。

Shanai de ichiban kakko ii no wa, yappari boku desu yo ne. Nimai-me da shi ne. / Shīn.

Like, everybody knows I'm the best-looking guy in the office, right. You know, the leading man, no less. / Yeah, sure.

☞ Originally, the sound of silence. The word is drawn out when uttered.

soreja (それじゃ) **"given that"** I'm outa here, Later, See ya.

それじゃ、今日は先に帰るよ。君たちは残業が好きだから文句はないだろう？

Soreja, kyō wa saki ni kaeru yo. Kimi-tachi wa zangyō ga suki da kara monku wa nai darō?

Catch you guys later. I'm outa here. You all don't mind stickin' around 'n puttin' in some overtime, right?

☞ An abbreviation of *sore de wa*. Among friends or peers.

un (うん) **"uh-huh"** Right, Yeah, I hear what you're saying.

正しいお返事は『うん』じゃなくて『はい』でしょう？／うん。

Tadashii ohenji wa "un" ja nakute "hai" deshō? / Un.

It's "yes," not "uh-huh." You got that? / Uh-huh.

☞ Used as a response to being called, as a sign of agreement with what is being said, or as an indication that one is paying attention to the conversation and is encouraging the speaker to continue.

ussō (ウッソー) **"lie"** Come on; no kidding; no shit; oh yeah?; really; you don't say.

おれ、マドンナと同じホテルに泊まっちゃった。／ウッソー。

Ore, Madonna to onaji hoteru ni tomatchatta. / Ussō.

Can you dig it? I stayed in the same hotel as Madonna! / You what?

☞ A corruption of *uso*. Used primarily by young women.

yai (やい) **"hey"** Hey you, yo, you there.

ヤイ、貴様！おれにぶつかっておいて謝りもしないつもりかよ。

Yai, kisama! Ore ni butsukatte oite ayamari mo shinai tsumori ka yo.

Hey, what's the big idea, buddy? Gonna bump into me and not even say you're sorry?

☞ Vulgar, hostile male usage. *Yaiyai* is even more emphatic.

yarū (ヤルー) **"(that's) doing it"** Far out, right on, that's cool.

あいつが去年書いた小説、直木賞の候補だってさ。／ヤルー。

Aitsu ga kyonen kaita shōsetsu, Naoki-shō no kōho datte sa. / Yarū.

Dude's novel was up for the Naoki Prize last year. / He's hot, man.

☞ From the verb *yaru*. Used by others when someone accomplishes something extraordinary. Accent clearly on last phoneme. Used by young people.

yattā (ヤッター) **"(that's) done it"** Alright, far out, outasight, yes.

ヤッター！懸賞クイズで「パリ10日間の旅」が当たったのよ。

Yattā! Kenshō-kuizu de "Pari tōka-kan no tabi" ga atatta no yo.

I did it! I entered this contest and won a ten-day vacation in Paris.

☞ From the verb *yaru*.

yoisho (よいしょ) **"heave-ho"** Here we go, heave, put your shoulder into it.

よいしょ！この箱をトラックに積んだら引っ越し完了だ。

Yoisho! Kono hako o torakku ni tsundara hikkoshi kanryō da.

Up she goes! Get this box loaded in the truck and I'll be done moving.

☞ When lifting something heavy or beginning something.

zamāmiro (ざまあ見ろ) **"look at the sight"** Serves you (him, her, etc.) right; take that; so there; how do you like them apples; stuff that in your pipe and smoke it.

ざまあ見ろ。勉強しないで遊んでばかりいるから落第したんだ。

Zamāmiro. Benkyō shinai de asonde bakari iru kara rakudai shita n' da.

Serves you right. You flunked 'cause all you ever did was fuck around. You never even cracked the books.

☞ *Zama* (a corruption of *sama*) refers to some poor, pathetic condition or state of affairs. More standard is *zama o miro* (様を見ろ).

Slang-Forming Prefixes and Suffixes:
Laying into 'em

PREFIXES

baka- (ばか／馬鹿) Attached prefixally to nouns and adjectives, imparts sense of extremity. May be used abusively. Vulgar. Original meaning is stupidity or a stupid person.

baka-dekai (ばかでかい) Ⓐ Huge, immense, lunking, monster, whopping.

ドミノスのピザはばかでかいから、一人じゃ食べきれないわよ。

Dominosu no piza wa baka-dekai kara, hitori ja tabekirenai wa yo.

Domino's pizzas are so humongous, I couldn't possibly eat one all by myself.

☞ Also, more emphatically, *baka-dekkai. Dekai* is colloquial for *ōkii.*

baka-sawagi (バカ騒ぎ) Ⓝ A bash, ruckus, wingdinger; raising hell, raising the roof.

昨日、ゼミのコンパでバカ騒ぎして、今朝はひどい二日酔いだよ。

Kinō, zemi no konpa de baka-sawagi shite, kesa wa hidoi futsuka-yoi da yo.

I partied hearty with a bunch of people from my seminar last night and now I've got this rip-roaring hangover.

☞ *Sawagi* is from *sawagu* (to raise a ruckus).

baka-teinei (バカ丁寧) Ⓐ Overly polite, polite to a fault.

お客様にバカ丁寧な説明をするのは、かえって失礼になるわよ。

Okyaku-sama ni baka-teinei na setsumei o suru no wa, kaette shitsurei ni naru wa yo.

If you overdo the politeness (bend over backwards) when explaining things to customers, you can end up by insulting them.

baka-uke (バカうけ) ⓃⒶ (Be) priceless, a riot, a scream.

彼の話はとてもおかしくて、まわりの人はいつもバカうけなの。

Kare no hanashi wa totemo okashikute, mawari no hito wa itsumo baka-uke na no.

His stories are such a crack-up that he's always got everybody rolling in the aisles.

☞ *Uke* (reception) is from *ukeru* (受ける).

baka-yasu (バカ安) N Cost next to nothing, super cheap.

東京―パリ間の往復航空券がバカ安で、10万5千円だったよ。

Tōkyō-Pari–kan no ōfuku–kōkū-ken ga baka-yasu de, jū-man go-sen'en datta yo.

Tokyo-Paris round trip for a hundred and five thousand yen was a real steal.

buchi- (ぶち／打ち) Attached prefixally to verb, it acts as an emphatic and may impart a sense of hitting or striking. Depending on the verb to which it is attached, it may change to either *bun-* or *bu'-*. From *butsu* (a corruption of *utsu*), the primary meaning of which is to hit.

buchiageru (ぶちあげる) V Tout, ballyhoo.

あの知事候補は大阪遷都論をぶちあげたけど、実現は不可能だ。

Ano chiji-kōho wa Ōsaka–sento-ron o buchiageta kedo, jitsugen wa fu-kanō da.

The gubernatorial candidate was touting some grandiose scheme to move the capital to Osaka, but there's no way it'll ever come to pass.

☞ Originally, to take away, snatch away.

buchiataru (ぶちあたる) V Run into, confront, face (a problem).

資金上の問題にぶちあたって、社長は新会社設立を断念したよ。

Shikin-jō no mondai ni buchiatatte, shachō wa shin-gaisha–setsuritsu o dannen shita yo.

The president had to give up his plans to start a new company when he ran into financial difficulties.

buchikamasu (ぶちかます) V Smack (ram) into; lay into, open up on.

けんかで勝つには、黙って先に一発ぶちかますだけでいいんだ。

Kenka de katsu ni wa, damatte saki ni ippatsu buchikamasu dake de ii n' da.

If you want to win a fight, all you've gotta do is get in the first licks (sucker punch the guy).

☞ *Kamasu* (originally the causative form of *kuu* [*kuwaseru*], meaning to force someone to eat) is colloquial for "to say, do, or let someone have it" (here in the latter sense). The entry term is originally from sumo wrestling, where it meant to hit one's opponent in the chest with one's head at the *tachiai*.

buchikomu (ぶちこむ／ぶち込む) V Throw something or someone into; shoot, blast.

警察は日本中のチンピラを、みんな刑務所にぶちこむべきだわ。

Keisatsu wa Nihon-jū no chinpira o, minna keimu-sho ni buchikomu beki da wa.

The cops oughta throw all the punks in Japan in prison where they belong.

おれの22口径で、おまえさんの頭にぶちこんでやろうか？

Ore no nijūni-kōkei de, omae-san no atama ni buchikonde yarō ka?

I gotta good notion to blow your fuckin' brains out with my 22.

buchikorosu (ぶち殺す) V Blow away, off, kill, waste, whack.

ぶち殺すなんて、ぶっそうなことというなよ。落ちつけよな。

Buchikorosu nante, bussō na koto iu na yo. Ochitsuke yo na.

You're talking some bad shit there, man, offing the dude and all. Chill out.

buchikowasu (ぶち壊す) V

1. Smash, bust (up).

ツッパリの生徒は、学校の窓ガラスをぶち壊すのが趣味なのね。

Tsuppari no seito wa, gakkō no madogarasu o buchikowasu no ga shumi na no ne.

Juvies sure get off breaking windows at school.

2. Sabotage (negotiations), trash, sink (a plan), smash (a plot).

首相暗殺計画をぶち壊すには、警察に密告する以外方法がない。

Shushō-ansatsu–keikaku o buchikowasu ni wa, keisatsu ni mikkoku suru igai hōhō ga nai.

The only way to bust up the plot to assassinate the prime minister is to tip off the cops.

buchimakeru (ぶちまける) V

1. Dump out.

階段で転んで、ハンドバッグの中身を全部ぶちまけちゃったの。

Kaidan de koronde, handobaggu no nakami o zenbu buchimakechatta no.

I fell on the stairs and everything spilled out of my purse.

2. Spill (one's guts out), blurt (everything) out.

昨日、友人に会社への不満をぶちまけて、少しせいせいしたよ。

Kinō, yūjin ni kaisha e no fuman o buchimakete, sukoshi seisei shita yo.

I feel a lot better since I opened up to a friend about all the problems I've been having at work.

☞ *Makeru* is "to scatter."

buchinomesu (ぶちのめす) V Flatten, beat the shit out of, pound.

うちの店で万引きするやつは、だれだろうとぶちのめしてやる。

Uchi no mise de manbiki suru yatsu wa, dare darō to buchinomeshite yaru.

If I catch anybody shoplifting at the store, I don't care who it is, I'm gonna beat the living daylights out of 'em.

☞ *Nomesu* is the transitive form of *nomeru*, to fall forward, to fall on all fours.

bukkakeru (ぶっかける) V Splash into (over), pour into (over).

ごはんにみそ汁をぶっかけるのは、行儀が悪いからやめろよな。

Gohan ni misoshiru o bukkakeru no wa, gyōgi ga warui kara yamero yo na.

Pouring miso soup over your rice is so uncouth. Cut it out, okay?

bunnageru (ぶん投げる) V Chuck, heave, sling, throw hard.

あいつは柔道二段だから、大男だってぶん投げるのは簡単なことだ。

Aitsu wa jūdō nidan da kara, ōotoko datte bunnageru no wa kantan na koto da.

Guy's got a second-degree black belt in judo, so it's no sweat for him to send some guy flying, no matter how big he is.

bunnaguru (ぶん殴る) V Bash, belt, hit, paste, pound, pulverize, smash.

訳もなく生徒をぶん殴るような教師は、教育委員会に通報しよう。

Wake mo naku seito o bunnaguru yō na kyōshi wa, kyōiku–iin-kai ni tsūhō shiyō.

Any damn teacher who smacks a student for no good reason oughta be reported to the board of education.

bunmawasu (ぶん回す) V Swing hard.

バットをぶん回すだけじゃ、ボールに当たらないよ。狙うんだ。

Batto o bunmawasu dake ja, bōru ni ataranai yo. Nerau n' da.

You're never gonna hit the ball just swinging at it as hard as you can. You've gotta keep your eye on it.

butchakeru (ぶっちゃける) V Speak honestly, be frank, hold nothing back.

ぶっちゃけた話、妻から離婚したいと言われて悩んでいるんだ。

Butchaketa hanashi, tsuma kara rikon shitai to iwarete nayande iru n' da.

To tell the truth, I'm kind of at a loss what to do since my wife's given me my walking papers.

☞ Corruption of *buchiakeru* (*uchiakeru*), *akeru* meaning to open up.

butchigiru (ぶっちぎる) V

1. Tear up, tear apart, rip up, rip apart.

酔った勢いでけんかして、相手のシャツをぶっちぎっちゃった。

Yotta ikioi de kenka shite, aite no shatsu o butchigitchatta.

Got in a drunken brawl with some guy and ripped his shirt up pretty bad.

2. [Horse racing, etc.] win easily, walk away from.

日本ダービーでは、ミカドが三馬身の差をつけてぶっちぎった。

Nihon-dābī de wa, Mikado ga sanbashin no sa o tsukete butchigitta.

Mikado made it look easy taking the Japan Derby, winning by three lengths.

☞ *Chigiru* meaning to tear up into small pieces.

bukkiru (ぶっきる) V Cut, slash.

宮本武蔵が刀で人をぶっきるときは、すごい迫力だっただろう。

Miyamoto Musashi ga katana de hito o bukkiru toki wa, sugoi haku-ryoku datta darō.

It must have really been something to see Musashi Miyamoto slash the shit out of an opponent with his sword.

bukkorosu (ぶっ殺す) V Grease, kill, off, waste, whack, zap.

あの男、結婚詐欺師だったの。今度見つけたらぶっ殺してやるわ。

Ano otoko, kekkon–sagi-shi datta no. Kondo mitsuketara bukkoro-shite yaru wa.

He said he wanted to marry me, but it was all just a big fraud. I swear I'll kill him if I ever see him again.

buppanasu (ぶっぱなす) V Fire (a gun); rip off (a fart).

暴力団の抗争事件でピストルをぶっぱなした男が逮捕された。

Bōryoku-dan no kōsō-jiken de pisutoru o buppanashita otoko ga tai-ho sareta.

The guy who fired off a pistol in the incident between rival gangs was arrested.

お前、よくも人前に屁をぶっぱなすもんだ。

Omae, yoku mo hitomae ni he o buppanasu mon da.

How can you go around cutting the cheese in front of people like that?

☞ *-Panasu* is *hanasu* (放す), to fire a shot or arrow.

buttakuru (ぶったくる) V

1. Appropriate, grab, liberate, take.

誘拐で身の代金をぶったくる計画になんか、とても協力できない。

Yūkai de minoshiro-kin o buttakuru keikaku ni nanka, totemo kyōryoku dekinai.

No way I'm going to have anything to do with a scheme to get ransom money by kidnapping someone.

2. Rip off, charge outrageous prices, overcharge, see someone coming.

赤坂のバーで飲んだら、ビール1本で2万円もぶったくられた。

Akasaka no bā de nondara, bīru ippon de ni-man'en mo buttakura-reta.

I got ripped off for 20,000 yen for one bottle of beer when I went to this bar in Akasaka.

☞ The primary meaning of *takuru* is to take for one's own.

buttamageru (ぶったまげる) Ⓥ Nearly shit, be floored, be blown away.

愛人の家に妻が押しかけてきたときは、本当にぶったまげた。

Aijin no ie ni tsuma ga oshikakete kita toki wa, hontō ni buttamageta.

I nearly shit my pants when my wife barged in on us at my girl-friend's place.

☞ *Tamageru* (魂消る) is understood to mean literally "the spirit disappears (in amazement)." *Keru* is a corruption of *kieru*. Vulgar.

buttaoreru (ぶっ倒れる) Ⓥ Crash and burn, collapse, crash to the floor.

事故の知らせを聞いたとき、ママはぶっ倒れたの。

Jiko no shirase o kiita toki, mama wa buttaoreta no.

Mom keeled over when she heard about the accident.

ぶっ倒れるまで働くなんて、あんたばかだわ。死んじゃうわよ。

Buttaoreru made hataraku nante, anta baka da wa. Shinjau wa yo.

It's crazy to keep working until you drop in your tracks. You're going to end up killing yourself.

buttaosu (ぶっ倒す) Ⓥ Drop, bring down, knock down.

おれは、強烈な右ストレートで相手をぶっ倒してKO勝ちした。

Ore wa, kyōretsu na migi-sutorēto de aite o buttaoshite kēō-gachi shita.

I dropped the sucker with a big right straight and won by a KO.

buttataku (ぶったたく) Ⓥ Pound, beat up on.

子供が言うことを聞かないときは、お尻をぶったたくのが一番。

Kodomo ga iu koto o kikanai toki wa, oshiri o buttataku no ga ichi-ban.

The best thing you can do when your kids don't listen to you is give them a good spanking (whipping, licking).

多国籍軍は、猛烈な空爆でイラクをぶったたいて戦争に勝った。

Takokuseki-gun wa, mōretsu na kūbaku de Iraku o buttataite sensō ni katta.

The coalition forces pounded Iraq into submission with fierce bombing raids.

buttobasu (ぶっ飛ばす) V

1. Blast something a long way, hit the long ball, launch one.

現役時代の小林は、場外ホームランをぶっ飛ばす選手だったね。

Gen'eki-jidai no Kobayashi wa, jōgai-hōmuran o buttobasu senshu datta ne.

Kobayashi really used to knock 'em outa the park when he was playing.

2. Knock someone senseless.

弟をいじめるやつは、だれだろうとオレがぶっ飛ばすぞ。

Otōto o ijimeru yatsu wa, dare darō to ore ga buttobasu zo.

I'm going to pound anyone who picks on my little brother, anyone!

3. [Of a car, motorcycle, etc.] step on it, open it up, punch it.

おれのフェラーリで中央高速をぶっ飛ばせば、甲府まで30分だ。

Ore no Ferāri de Chūō Kōsoku o buttobaseba, Kōfu made sanjuppun da.

Thirty minutes, man! That's all it takes to get to Kofu in my Ferrari when I put the pedal to the metal on the Chuo Expressway.

buttobu (ぶっ飛ぶ) V

1. To fly off, be sent sailing.

今朝隣の家でガス爆発があって、屋根がぶっ飛んじゃったんだ。

Kesa tonari no ie de gasu-bakuhatsu ga atte, yane ga buttonjatta n' da.

The gas explosion at my neighbor's house this morning blew the roof off.

2. Fly, go (someplace fast), haul ass, make good time.

最寄りの病院へ救急車でぶっ飛んで行っても、2時間はかかる。

Moyori no byōin e kyūkyū-sha de buttonde itte mo, ni-jikan wa kakaru.

It takes two full hours to get to the nearest hospital in an ambulance even if you really haul ass.

3. Disappear completely, be finished, be curtains for.

もし部下の横領が発覚したら、部長の首もぶっ飛ぶのは確実だ。

Moshi buka no ōryō ga hakkaku shitara, buchō no kubi mo buttobu no wa kakujitsu da.

Make no mistake about it, if one of the guys at the office gets caught with his hand in the till, the boss'll get the ax, too.

☞ Vulgar. Used by men.

buttōsu (ぶっ通す) Ⓥ

1. Pierce, go through.

ピアスのために、耳たぶをぶっ通して穴をあけるなんていやよ。

Piasu no tame ni, mimitabu o buttōshite ana o akeru nante iya yo.

No way I'm gonna go poking a hole in my earlobe just so I can wear pierced earrings.

2. Keep on doing (something).

営業部が昼食抜きで会議をぶっ通すなんて、珍しいことなんだ。

Eigyō-bu ga chūshoku-nuki de kaigi o buttōsu nante, mezurashii koto nan da.

It's unusual for the sales department to stay in a meeting straight through lunch.

3. Tear down, knock down (a wall); connect (two rooms).

隣の会議室もぶっ通して大宴会場にすれば1、000人は収容できます。

Tonari no kaigi-shitsu mo buttōshite dai–enkai-jō ni sureba sen-nin wa shūyō dekimasu.

If you knock out the wall and connect the conference room next door, you can make a banquet hall that'll hold a thousand people.

do- (ど) Attached prefixally to nouns and adjectives, *do* imparts a sense of vulgarity, abusiveness, and extremity. Used widely in the Kansai district.

do-aho (ドアホ) Ⓝ A complete fool, numskull, blockhead, dimwit, stupid shit, dumbfuck.

おれの上司はドアホで、自分の責任が全然わかってないんだよ。

Ore no jōshi wa do-aho de, jibun no sekinin ga zenzen wakatte 'nai n' da yo.

My boss is such an airhead that he doesn't even know what he's responsible for.

do-busu (ドブス) Ⓝ An ugly girl, a dog, pig, skag, two-bagger.

あいつみたいなドブスは、銀行の窓口業務には向いていないね。

Aitsu mitai na do-busu wa, ginkō no madoguchi-gyōmu ni wa muite inai ne.

Any gal that's as plug-ugly as she is shouldn't be working as a bank teller.

do-erai (どえらい) Ⓐ

1. Great, famous, big.

ひょんなことから、中国のどえらい学者に会うはめになったよ。

Hyonna koto kara, Chūgoku no do-erai gakusha ni au hame ni natta yo.

I had to met some big-whig Chinese scholar just by a fluke.

2. Unexpectedly awful; really great, in a terrible fix.

先生の原稿をどっかに置き忘れた。どえらいことしてしまった。

Sensei no genkō o dokka ni okiwasureta. Do-erai koto shite shimatta.

I went and left the teacher's manuscript somewhere. Now I'm really in for it.

☞ Both meanings vulgar.

do-gitsui (どぎつい) Ⓐ Disgusting, overwhelming, too much.

マキナニーの最新小説には、かなりどぎつい描写が多いらしい。

Makinarī no saishin-shōsetsu ni wa, kanari do-gitsui byōsha ga ōi rashii.

I hear McInerney's latest novel's chock-full of some pretty graphic descriptions.

☞ Here *kitsui* (*-gitsui*) means extreme, awful.

do-hade (ど派手) Ⓐ Garish, gaudy, loud, screaming.

ど派手なデザインの服でも、君ならすごく似合うよ。

Do-hade na dezain no fuku de mo, kimi nara sugoku niau yo.

Even flashy clothes would look really great on you.

do-heta (ど下手) Ⓐ Bad, terrible, as bad as they come.

おまえみたいにカラオケがど下手なやつ、他に見たことないぞ。

Omae mitai ni karaoke ga do-heta na yatsu, hoka ni mita koto nai zo.

Your karaoke is the pits, man. I've never heard anyone as horrible as you are.

do-kechi (どけち) Ⓝ A cheapskate, skinflint, tightass. Ⓐ (Super) cheap, stingy, tight.

あたしの彼はどケチで、夕食は吉田屋の牛丼以外食べないのよ。

Atashi no kare wa do-kechi de, yūshoku wa Yoshida-ya no gyūdon igai tabenai no yo.

My boyfriend's such a tightwad that he won't eat anything but the beef bowl at Yoshidaya's for dinner.

do-konjō (ど根性) Ⓝ Backbone, grit, gumption, guts, heart, moxy, spunk.

将来の夢に向かってどんな試練にも堪えるのが、男のど根性だ。

Shōrai no yume ni mukatte donna shiren ni mo taeru no ga, otoko no do-konjō da.

Overcoming all obstacles to achieve your dreams, that's what being a real man means.

☞ Originally, but no longer, abusive.

do-mannaka (ど真ん中) N Right in the middle, smack dab in the middle.

友達とダーツをしたら、全部ど真ん中に命中して優勝したんだ。

Tomodachi to dātsu o shitara, zenbu do-mannaka ni meichū shite yūshō shita n' da.

I was playing darts with some of my buddies, and I hit the bull's-eye with every shot and won.

do-shirōto (ど素人) N A rank amateur, beginner, rookie.

ど素人が株売買に手を出せば、いいカモにされて損するだけさ。

Do-shirōto ga kabu-baibai ni te o daseba, ii kamo ni sarete sonsuru dake sa.

Someone who starts playing the market without knowing which way is up is bound to get fleeced.

do-wasure (度忘れ) N Forgetting something momentarily. V (suru) Letting something slip one's mind, have something on the tip of one's tongue.

カポーティーのあの小説の題名なんだっけ。度忘れしちゃった。

Kapōtī no ano shōsetsu no daimei nan da kke. Do-wasure shichatta.

What was the name of that novel by Capote? It's slipped my mind.

fun- (ふん) Attached prefixally to a verb, *fun* imparts a sense of violence. A corruption of *fumi-*, from *fumu* (踏む; to step on, to take a step).

fundakuru (ふんだくる) V

1. Grab, rip off, snatch.

老人からお金をふんだくるようなやつは人間じゃないわ。

Rōjin kara okane o fundakuru yō na yatsu wa ningen ja nai wa.

Anyone who would snatch money out of the hands of old people is really subhuman.

2. Gouge, jack up the price, overcharge, rip off.

訪問販売で英語の教材を買ったら、50万円もふんだくられた。

Hōmon-hanbai de Eigo no kyōzai o kattara, gojū-man'en mo fundakurareta.

I got ripped off for five hundred thousand yen when I bought this English course from a door-to-door salesman.

☞ *Takuru (dakuru)* is to take for one's own. See also *buttakuru*.

funjibaru (ふん縛る) Ⓥ Tie up (tightly).

パパは捕まえた空き巣をふん縛って、警察に突きだしてやった。

Papa wa tsukamaeta akisu o funjibatte, keisatsu ni tsukidashite yatta.

Dad hog-tied the cat burglar he caught and turned him over to the police.

☞ *Shibaru (jibaru)* is to tie.

fun-zukamaeru (ふん捕まえる) Ⓥ Bag, catch, collar, grab.

パンティー泥棒をふん捕まえるまで、交替で見張りをすべきね。

Pantī-dorobō o fun-zukamaeru made, kōtai de mihari o subeki ne.

We ought to take turns keeping watch until we nail the guy who's going around stealing panties.

hin- (ひん) Attached prefixally to a verb, *hin* is the emphatic form of *hiku* (pull) and intensifies the verb.

hinmagaru (ひん曲がる) Ⓥ Be all bent (twisted) up.

トラックが衝突して、家の前のガードレールがひん曲がったぜ。

Torakku ga shōtotsu shite, ie no mae no gādorēru ga hinmagatta ze.

Some truck ran into the guardrail in front of my house and bent it all to hell.

夏にゴミの処理場へいくと、悪臭で鼻がひん曲がりそうになるよ。

Natsu ni gomi no shori-jō e iku to, akushū de hana ga hinmagarisō ni naru yo.

Go to the dump during the summer and the stink practically bends your nose out of shape.

hinmageru (ひん曲げる) Ⓥ Twist (bend) something out of shape, distort.

ユリ・ゲラーは超能力でスプーンをひん曲げる、と有名だった。

Yuri Gerā wa chō-nōryoku de supūn o hinmageru, to yūmei datta.

Uri Geller was famous for being able to bend spoons through supernatural power.

芸能週刊誌はいつも事実をひん曲げて、うそばかり書くのよね。

Geinō–shūkan-shi wa itsumo jijitsu o hinmagete, uso bakari kaku no yo ne.

Oh, those supermarket tabloids are always twisting the facts and telling a bunch of lies.

hinmekuru (ひんめくる) Ⓥ Turn (a page) over violently.

かたっぱしから辞書をひんめくるのが、語学の勉強ではないよ。

Katappashi kara jisho o hinmekuru no ga, gogaku no benkyō de wa nai yo.

There's a lot more to studying a language than just flipping through the pages of a dictionary.

hinnuku (ひん抜く) ⚡Ⓥ Pluck out, jerk out.

暑いなあ。冷たいビールの栓をすぽんとひん抜いてグーッと飲みたいぜ。

Atsui nā. Tsumetai bīru no sen o supon to hinnuite gū'tto nomitai ze.

Jeez, it's hot. I could dig poppin' a few tops and chuggin' a brew or two.

ike- (いけ) This emphatic prefix is both abusive and vulgar. The origins are unclear. One of several possibilities suggested is a corruption of *yokei* (余計; superfluous).

ike-shāshā (いけしゃあしゃあ) Ⓐ Maddeningly brazen, bold as brass, cheeky, smart-ass.

この忙しい時期にいけしゃあしゃあと休暇なんかよく取れるね。

Kono isogashii jiki ni ikeshāshā to kyūka nanka yoku toreru ne.

I can't get over how he doesn't think anything of taking time off now when we're so busy.

ike-sukanai (いけ好かない) Ⓐ Creepy, lousy, low down, skuzzy, slimey, be a sleazeball, yucky.

あの人は親切だけど、何か企んでるみたいでいけ好かないなあ。

Ano hito wa shinsetsu da kedo, nani ka takurande 'ru mitai de ike-sukanai nā.

Oh, he's nice enough alright, but there's a sleazy side to him that gives you the feeling he's got something up his sleeve.

☞ *Sukanai* is the negative form of *suku*, from which is derived the common *suki*.

ike-zūzūshii (いけずうずうしい) Ⓐ Cheeky, have one helluva nerve, nervy, shameless.

よその家の冷蔵庫を黙って開けるなんていけずうずうしい人ね。

Yoso no ie no reizō-ko o damatte akeru nante ike-zūzūshii hito ne.

You've got some nerve to just walk right into someone's house and dig around in their refrigerator.

kuso- (くそ) Attached prefixally to nouns and adjectives, imparts a vulgar sense of condemnation as well as extremity.

Original meaning is "shit."

kuso-babā (くそばばあ) Ⓝ Bag, biddy, bitch, hen.

あたしはあんたの母親で、くそばばあなんかじゃありませんよ。

Atashi wa anta no haha-oya de, kusobabā nanka ja arimasen yo.

I'm your mother, not some old hag you can just talk to any way you want. / I'm your mother, and I won't have you calling me as an old bitch.

☞ About any woman, regardless of age, older than the speaker.

kuso-bōzu (くそ坊主) Ⓝ

1. [Of a Buddhist priest] a fuckin' priest.

あの寺のくそ坊主、境内に貸しビル建てて金儲けするつもりだ。

Ano tera no kuso-bōzu, keidai ni kashibiru tatete kanemōke suru tsumori da.

Now that fuckin' priest is puttin' up a building right on the temple grounds so he can rent it out and make a bundle.

2. [Of a young boy] an anklebiter, a brat, crumbcrusher, rug rat.

くそ坊主、ガラスを割ったのはおまえだなあ。どこの家のガキだ。

Kuso-bōzu, garasu o watta no wa omae da nā. Doko no ie no gaki da.

So, you're the one who broke the window, you little bugger! Where do you live, anyway?

☞ Priests and little boys are associated by means of the shaven pates of the former and the close-cropped heads of the latter (mandatory before World War II).

kuso-dokyō (くそ度胸) Ⓝ Balls, guts, daring, foolhardiness.

モトクロスのライダーになるなら、くそ度胸がなければだめだ。

Motokurosu no raidā ni naru nara, kuso-dokyō ga nakereba dame da.

You've really gotta have balls to ride motocross.

kuso-jijī (くそじじい) Ⓝ An old bugger, old fart, geezer.

くそじじい、ブツブツ文句ばっかり言わないで自分でやればどうだ。

Kuso-jijī, butsubutsu monku bakkari iwanai de jibun de yareba dō da.

Quit grousing, you old geezer, and do it yourself.

☞ About any man, regardless of age, who is older than the speaker.

kuso-jikara (くそ力) Ⓝ Brute strength, uncommon strength, the strength of an ox.

火事で気が動転したせいか、くそ力でピアノも運びだしたんだ。

Kaji de ki ga dōten shita sei ka, kuso-jikara de piano mo hakobidashita n' da.

I guess the fire must have set me off or something, the way I did this superman thing and carried the piano out of the house.

☞ Also *baka-jikara*.

kuso-majime (くそまじめ) Ⓐ Ridiculously serious, all work and no play, no fun.

あいつ、教授の言う冗談までノートに書くほどくそまじめなの。

Aitsu, kyōju no iu jōdan made nōto ni kaku hodo kuso-majime na no.

Guy's such a grind (pencil, neck), he even takes down the prof's jokes.

kuso-omoshiroku (mo) nai (くそおもしろく[も]ない) Boring as hell, borrring.

卒業式で、学長はくそおもしろくもない話を1時間もしたんだ。

Sotsugyō-shiki de, gakuchō wa kuso-omoshiroku mo nai hanashi o ichi-jikan mo shita n' da.

The president bored everybody stiff for a full hour during commencement.

kuso-oyaji (くそおやじ) Ⓝ Old man, pops.

このくそおやじ、もうそろそろ帰ってくれよ。

Kono kuso-oyaji, mō sorosoro kaette kure yo.

Why don't you get your butt outa here, Pops.

☞ Used disparagingly of a man, middle-aged or older. The word *oyaji* itself refers primarily to one's own father in an affectionate way or humbly in front of others. An extended meaning (as above) is that of any middle-aged or older man, in either an friendly or belittling tone.

kuso-samui (くそさむい) Ⓐ Colder'n hell, colder'n a witch's tit.

こんな氷雨の降るくそ寒い日には、家でごろごろしていたいなあ。

Konna hisame no furu kuso-samui hi ni wa, ie de gorogoro shite itai nā.

I sure wish I could just lie around the house on days like this, when the hawk's out and there's a freezing rain.

o'- (おっ) A corruption of *oshi* (押し; push), this vulgar verbal prefix intensifies the meaning of the verb.

okkabuseru (おっかぶせる) Ⓥ

1. Stick on, slam (down) on, slap on.

犬に帽子をおっかぶせて、服まで着せようなんて、ばかげてるわ。

Inu ni bōshi o okkabusete, fuku made kiseyō nante, bakagete 'ru wa.

Sticking a hat on a dog and dressing it up in clothes, how stupid!

2. [Of responsibility] place on, lay on, sluff off on.

自分の責任を部下におっかぶせるなら、課長の資格なんかない。

Jibun no sekinin o buka ni okkabuseru nara, kachō no shikaku nanka nai.

You're not qualified to be section chief if you're always shifting the blame for everything onto the people under you.

oppajimeru (おっ始める) Ⓥ Start, get it on.

大変だよ。国境付近で政府軍と人民軍が戦争をおっ始めたって。

Taihen da yo. Kokkyō-fukin de seifu-gun to jinmin-gun ga sensō o oppajimeta tte.

Bad news, man. Word is that the army and the militia are slugging it along the border.

oppirogeru (おっぴろげる) Ⓥ Spread, open wide.

若い男と言えども、電車の中で股をおっぴろげて座るのは感心しないね。

Wakai otoko to iedomo, densha no naka de mata o oppirogete suwaru no wa kanshin shinai ne.

I don't care if it is some young stud or not, I'm not exactly thrilled when they sit in the train with their legs spread all over the place.

opporidasu (おっぽりだす) Ⓥ

1. [Of things] throw out, chuck, toss; [of people] kick out.

おまえのような穀潰しは、この家からおっぽり出すからな。

Omae no yō na gokutsubushi wa, kono ie kara opporidasu kara na.

You're going to find yourself out on the street so fast your head spins, you no-good loafer.

2. Be fed up with something and quit doing it.

兄さんは宿題をおっぽり出して、どこかに遊びに行っちゃった。

Nīsan wa shukudai o opporidashite, doko ka ni asobi ni itchatta.

My big brother ODed on doing homework, so he just shined it and split.

☞ *Horidasu* (*-poridasu*) is a corruption of standard *hōridasu* (放り出す).

ottamageru (おったまげる) Ⓥ Be super surprised, blown away, thrown for a loop.

おったまげたなあ。君たちがそっくりなのは双子だったからか。

Ottamageta nā. Kimi-tachi ga sokkuri na no wa futago datta kara ka.

Blows my mind, man. Like, the reason you guys look so much alike is 'cause you're twins.

☞ See note to synonymous *buttamageru*, above.

ottateru (おったてる／おっ立てる) Ⓥ Build, put up.

あちこちに案内板をおったてても、客はひとりも来なかったわ。

Achikochi ni annai-ban o ottatete mo, kyaku wa hitori mo konakatta wa.

Not even one lousy customer came in even though we stuck signs up all over the place.

su'- (すっ) Emphatic prefix attached to nouns, verbs, and adjectives alike, indicating that a certain condition or state exceeds the normal. Primarily used in the Tokyo dialect. Often written 素, but this appears to be simply a homophonic kanji equivalent.

suppokasu (すっぽかす) Ⅴ

1. Stand someone up.

あの子と4時に会う約束だったのに、すっぽかされた。

Ano ko to yo-ji ni au yakusoku datta no ni, suppokasareta.

She and I were supposed to get together at 4:00, but the bitch stood me up.

2. Shine, let something slide.

あんたは自分の仕事をすっぽかして遊んでいるからだめなのよ。

Anta wa jibun no shigoto o suppokashite asonde iru kara dame na no yo.

It's your own fault for letting your work slide and fooling around all the time.

☞ *Hokasu (-pokasu; 放す)* is to throw away.

suttobokeru (すっとぼける) Ⅴ Feign ignorance, fake it.

山田君なら、失敗してもすっとぼけるのが上手だから大丈夫。

Yamada-kun nara, shippai shite mo suttobokeru no ga jōzu da kara daijōbu.

Yamada'll be alright. Guy's a genius at playing dumb.

suttobu (すっ飛ぶ) Ⅴ Go flying; fly out.

裁断機に触れると指がすっ飛ぶから、十分気をつけてください。

Saidan-ki ni fureru to yubi ga suttobu kara, jūbun ki o tsukete kudasai.

Be real careful. Touch that cutter wrong and that's the last you'll see of your finger.

SUFFIXES

-kō (公) Suffixed to nouns describing people or animals, *-ko* adds a sense of familiarity or scorn, depending on the situation. From its original meaning of "unbiased" or "fair," it has taken on a number of other meanings, among which are "public," its use as an affix of respect for nobility or elders ("your honor"), to the ironic meaning dealt with here ("your high muckamuck," say).

ame-kō (アメ公) N Yank, Yankee, fuckin' American.

おい、アメ公！箸なんか無理して使わないで、フォーク使えよ。

Oi, ame-kō! Hashi nanka muri shite tsukawanaide, fōku tsukae yo.

Hey, Yank! Don't you think it's about time you stopped fiddling around with those chopsticks and use something you can handle, like a fork maybe?
☞ *Ame* is short for *Amerika*.

ete-kō (猿公) N A monkey, ape, simian.

エテ公の社会にも、人間の社会と同じような階層があるんだ。

Ete-kō no shakai ni mo, ningen no shakai to onaji yō na kaisō ga aru n' da.

Ape society has classes just like human society does.
☞ Originally written 得手 (with the primary meaning of forte, then by a devious route, a known but unnamed person or thing), the use of *ete* is said to have arisen from an aversion to using the normal word for monkey, *saru*, which is a homophone for "to depart."

ita-kō (イタ公) N A wop, dago, spic, guinea.

青山のサバティーニには、イタ公の客がいつもたくさん来てる。

Aoyama no Sabatīni ni wa, ita-kō no kyaku ga itsumo takusan kite 'ru.

There's always a bunch of wops at that restaurant Sabatini in Aoyama.
☞ *Ita* is short for *Itaria*.

pori-kō (ポリ公) N Cop, fuzz, pig.

駐車違反の取り締まりだけなら、ポリ公も気楽な商売だろうね。

Chūsha-ihan no torishimari dake nara, pori-kō mo kiraku na shōbai darō ne.

If all the pigs had to do was write parking tickets, they'd really be on the gravy train.
☞ *Pori* is shortened from *porisu* (or *porīsu*).

-kusai (くさい／臭い) Appended to a noun expressing some undesirable state of affairs, *-kusai* emphasizes the degree of undesirability. The original meaning is to stink or smell or be redolent of, deriving from *kusaru* (to rot), and thus suggests that the present situation has unpleasant similarities to the preceding nominal.

aho-kusai (あほくさい) Ⓐ Really dumb, hopelessly stupid, dumber 'n a box of rocks.

愛が薄れた、なんてあほくさいこと言ってないでメシにしよう。

Ai ga usureta, nante aho-kusai koto itte 'nai de meshi ni shiyō.

Don't give me that ridiculous shit about me not loving you anymore. Let's just eat, okay?

baka-kusai (ばかくさい) Ⓐ Ludicrous, outrageous, dumb, lamebrained, dippy.

一日中コピーするだけなんてばかくさい仕事はやりたくないわ。

Ichinichi-jū kopī suru dake nante baka-kusai shigoto wa yaritaku nai wa.

I don't want some stupid job where all you do is make copies all day.

don-kusai (どんくさい) Ⓐ Obtuse, foolish, doofus.

わざわざハワイに行って、風邪で寝ていたなんてどんくさいな。

Wazawaza Hawai ni itte, kaze de nete ita nante don-kusai na.

Go all the way to Hawaii and end up spending all your time in bed with a cold, how dumb can you get?

☞ *Don* (鈍) means dull, blunt, slow.

mendō-kusai (面倒臭い) Ⓐ Pesky, wicked, troublesome.

会社まで歩くのが面倒臭いからタクシーに乗ることにしよう。

Kaisha made aruku no ga mendō-kusai kara takushī ni noru koto ni shiyō.

Walking all the way to the office is too much of a hassle, man. Whadaya say we catch a cab?

☞ *Mendō* (the kanji are homophonic) is perhaps one of the most frequently used words in the Japanese vocabulary. It seems originally to have meant something not worth looking at, then something unsightly, and, here, that something is simply a lot of trouble.

-kuso (くそ) Attached to nouns and other parts of speech, the emphatic *-kuso* imparts a sense of scorn to the meaning of the compound it forms. The original meaning is "shit."

borokuso (ぼろくそ) Ⓝ Something absolutely useless or without value, not worth shit. Ⓐ (Criticize) severely.

徹夜までして書いた稟議書を課長からぼろくそにけなされた。

Tetsuya made shite kaita ringi-sho o kachō kara borokuso ni kenasareta.

My boss really cut up the petition that I stayed up all night writing.
☞ *Boro* means "rag."

hetakuso (へたくそ) Ⓝ Good-for-nothing, (something that) sucks. Ⓐ Awful, bad, terrible.

君の字はへたくそだなあ。もう少しきれいに書けないのかね。

Kimi no ji wa hetakuso da nā. Mō sukoshi kirei ni kakenai no ka ne.

Your handwriting really sucks. Can't you do something to improve it?

metakuso (めたくそ) Ⓐ Really bad, terrible; all over, up and down.

ぼくの好きな小説家の最新作を、新聞はめたくそに批評したよ。

Boku no suki na shōsetsu-ka no saishin-saku o, shinbun wa metakuso ni hihyō shita yo.

The newspapers ripped the latest novel by my favorite author to shreds.
☞ *Meta* means wildly, frenziedly, furiously.

yakekuso (やけくそ) Ⓝ Cowboy. Ⓐ Devil-may-care, rash.

彼女にふられ、ぼくはやけくそになってウイスキーをあおった。

Kanojo ni furare, boku wa yakekuso ni natte uisukī o aotta.

After my girlfriend dumped me, I didn't care what happened anymore and started hitting the juice pretty hard.
☞ *Yake* (burned) means that you are so burned up, frustrated, or put-out that you no longer care what happens and act accordingly.

-suke (すけ／助け) Appended to various parts of speech including nouns, *-suke* is used to create nicknames for people by nominalizing a characteristic trait. Originally a common appendage to masculine given names.

chibisuke (ちびすけ) Ⓝ Half-pint, peewee, pipsqueak, runt, shrimp, squirt, tiny.

あなた、3時15分になったらちびすけにミルク飲ませてちょうだいね。

Anata, san-ji jūgo-fun ni nattara chibisuke ni miruku nomasete chōdai ne.

You won't forget to give Junior his bottle at 3:15, will you, Honey?

☞ *Chibi* (used in much the same fashion as the entry word) is from the verb *chibiru* (to be worn down and become small). Used derogatorily of small people and, diminutively, of children and animals.

nebosuke (寝坊すけ) Ⓝ Sleepyhead.

もうお昼だって言うのに、寝坊すけの兄貴はまだベットの中だ。

Mō ohiru datte iu no ni, nebosuke no aniki wa mada betto no naka da.

It's noon already, and that sleepyhead brother of mine still can't seem to get out of bed.

☞ *Nebo* is shortened from *nebō*.

nomisuke (飲みすけ) Ⓝ A barfly, big (heavy) drinker, fish, juicer, lush.

おまえは飲みすけだから、注意しないとアル中になっちゃうよ。

Omae wa nomisuke da kara, chūi shinai to aruchū ni natchau yo.

You're such a boozer you'll end up turning into an alky if you don't watch it.

-tare (たれ／垂れ) Appended to nouns, *-tare* forms a derogatory term for any person considered to display a particular characteristic or condition. From the verb *tareru* (to hang down, drip down, to piss, shit, or fart).

ahotare (あほたれ) Ⓝ A (complete) fool, idiot, knucklehead, lunkhead, dumbshit.

店の金に手をつけるとは、このあほたれが。おまえはもう首だ。

Mise no kane ni te o tsukeru to wa, kono ahotare ga. Omae wa mō kubi da.

Got your hand in the till, huh, dipshit! You're outa here.

☞ Also *bakatare*.

kusottare (くそったれ) Ⓝ Shit-ass, asshole, dickhead, shithead.

文句があるのか、このくそったれ。一体、何様のつもりなんだ。

Monku ga aru no ka, kono kusottare. Ittai, nani-sama no tsumori nan da.

What's your problem, asswipe? Who the hell you think you are, anyway?

☞ Said despicably of someone as though they were incontinent.

shimittare (しみったれ) Ⓝ Last of the big-time spenders, a cheapskate, tightwad; cheap, stingy, tight-fisted.

愚痴ばかり言ってるあんなしみったれとは、さっさと別れろよ。

Guchi bakari itte 'ru anna shimittare to wa, sassa to wakarero yo.

The guy's a cronic complainer and a tightwad to boot. Give him his
walking papers and be done with him.

☞ The meaning of *shimi* is unclear.

unkotare (うんこたれ) N A child who shits his pants; an immature
adult, big baby.

どうしてトイレまでがまんできないの。困ったうんこたれね。

Dōshite toire made gaman dekinai no. Komatta unkotare ne.

Why do you have to go in your pants all the time? Can't you learn to
just hold it till you get to a toilet?

20才にもなって駄々をこねるなんて、あんたはそんなうんこたれな
の？

*Nijussai ni mo natte dada o koneru nante, anta wa sonna unkotare
na no?*

You big baby, you. Twenty and still acting like a spoiled brat.

☞ *Unko* is baby talk for feces.

Colloquial Phrases:
I Hate to Say It, But …

chū (ちゅう) Corruption of *to iu* (と言う). Used when talking to oneself or close friends. Not appropriate for use to one's superiors. Also *tsū* (つう): "Called, named; of."

こりゃなんちゅう絵なんだ。抽象的でさっぱりわかりゃしない。

Korya nan chū e nan da. Chūshō-teki de sappari wakarya shinai.

What's this painting called, anyway? It's so abstract I can't make head or tail out of it.

もう、わかったちゅうに。二度と浮気はしないから許してくれ。

Mō, wakatta chū ni. Nido to uwaki wa shinai kara yurushite kure.

Alright, already. I'm not gonna step out on you anymore, so just give me a break, will ya?

itcha nan da kedo (言っちゃなんだけど) An abbreviation of *itte wa nani da kedo*, meaning something like, "Saying (this), it may be something (you don't want to hear), but." Also *itchā nan da ga*: "I hate to say it, but; Sorry to say it, but; You're not going to like what I've got to say, but."

こう言っちゃなんだけど、あんたは頭が悪いから大学は無理だわ。

Kō itcha nan da kedo, anta wa atama ga warui kara daigaku wa muri da wa.

I hate to be the one to tell you, but you're just not smart enough to go to college.

言っちゃなんだけど、言わなきゃあんたは気がつかないでしょ？

Itcha nan da kedo, iwanakya anta wa ki ga tsukanai desho?

Far be it from me to criticize you, but if someone doesn't tell you, you'll just never figure it out yourself.

mon (もん) Corruption of *mono* (者). Preceded by a modifier: "Guy, gal, person."

ぼくのようなもんでも、自分の食べるものにはうるさいんですよ。

Boku no yō na mon de mo, jibun no tabemono ni wa urusai n' desu yo.

Even a guy like me's choosy about what he eats.

パパ、スパイダーマンは悪もんじゃない。正義の味方なんだよ。

Papa, Supaidāman wa waru-mon ja nai. Seigi no mikata nan da yo.

Come on, Dad. Spiderman's not a baddie. He's one of the good guys.

mon da (もんだ) Colloquial corruption of *mono da* (*mono* referring to an abstract entity). Preceded by a modifier, it appears at the end of a sentence expressing a sense of nostalgia, hope, deep impression, obviousness, or moralizing.

昔の子供は、みんな親の手伝いを嫌がらずにしたもんだぞ。

Mukashi no kodomo wa, minna oya no tetsudai o iyagarazu ni shita mon da zo.

Kids didn't used to moan and groan all the time about helping their parents.

老人の言うことは、人生の先輩として、よく聞いておくもんだ。

Rōjin no iu koto wa, jinsei no senpai toshite, yoku kiite oku mon da.

What old people have to say ought to be taken to heart as lessons in life from someone who's been there.

病弱だったあの子がよくここまで育ったもんだ。大したもんだ。

Byōjaku datta ano ko ga yoku koko made sodatta mon da. Taishita mon da.

For a child that was as sickly as she was, she's really hung in there. I'm impressed.

mon de (もんで) Colloquial corruption of *mono de*. Preceded by a modifier, it is used to explain or justify one's behavior.

女房が風邪で寝込んでいるもんで、今日は先に失礼しますよ。

Nyōbō ga kaze de nekonde iru mon de, kyō wa saki ni shitsurei shimasu yo.

The wife's a little under the weather with a cold, so I'm going to have to leave the office a little early today.

mon ka (もんか) Colloquial corruption of *mono ka*. Preceded by a modifier, it appears at the end of a sentence expressing either strong feelings of rejection or a rhetorical question one knows will be answered negatively: "No way, not on your life."

どんな試練にだって負けるもんか。

Donna shiren ni datte makeru mon ka.

I don't care what life throws at me, no way I'm knuckling under.

あいつは強情なやつだから、どんなに説教したって聞くもんか。

Aitsu wa gōjō na yatsu da kara, donna ni sekkyō shita tte kiku mon ka.

He's one hard-headed son-of-a-gun. You can talk yourself blue in the face, but it won't get you anywhere.

nantatte (なんたって／何たって) Abbreviated form of *nan to itta tte*, with a literal meaning such as "whatever said." Used for emphasis, often indicating preference for one thing over another: "After all; when you come down to it."

あたしはお寿司だったら、なんたってあわびが一番好きなんだ。

Atashi wa osushi dattara, nantatte awabi ga ichiban suki nan da.

There's no two ways about it. Abalone's my favorite when it comes to sushi.

あの子はなんたってまだ小学生よ。大人の話は理解できないわ。

Ano ko wa nantatte mada shōgaku-sei yo. Otona no hanashi wa rikai dekinai wa.

You can't expect him to understand what grownups are talking about. Remember, he's only in elementary school.

n' chi (んち) Abbreviated form of *no uchi (の家)*. Not used when addressing one's superiors: "One's house, place, pad, digs."

ぼくんちで宿題すませてから、おまえんちでゲームして遊ぼう。

Boku n' chi de shukudai sumasete kara, omae n'chi de gēmu shite asobō.

Let's go over to your house and play games after we do our homework at my place.

きみんちのお父さんは、いつも何時ごろに会社から帰るんだい。

Kimi n' chi no otōsan wa, itsumo nan-ji goro ni kaisha kara kaeru n' dai.

What time does that father of yours usually get home from work?

n' da (んだ) Corruption of *no da*. Appended to verbs as well as other parts of speech to emphasize cause, reason, the speaker's resolution or a demand made on someone by the speaker; it is not appropriate when addressing one's superiors.

パパは事故で死んだんだ。だから、もうこの世にはいないんだ。

Papa wa jiko de shinda n' da. Da kara, mō kono yo ni wa inai n' da.

My dad's not here anymore 'cause he died in an accident.

あたしは一生懸命勉強して、絶対にりっぱな看護婦になるんだ。

Atashi wa isshō-kenmei benkyō shite, zettai ni rippa na kango-fu ni naru n' da.

You'll see. I'm going to study as hard as I can and become a really good nurse someday.

必ずこの薬を飲むんだ。でなきゃ、君の病気は治らないんだ。

Kanarazu kono kusuri o nomu n' da. Denakya, kimi no byōki wa naoranai n' da.

You've gotta take this medicine. You'll never get better if you don't.

n' de (んで) Corruption of *no de*. Used by men: "'Cause, since, that's why."

ぼくの給料が安いんで、夫婦で共稼ぎをしてる。

Boku no kyūryō ga yasui n' de, fūfu de tomokasegi o shite 'ru.

My wife 'n I are both working 'cause my salary's so low.

赤ちゃんがもうじき生まれるんで、なんだか落ち着かないんだ。

Akachan ga mō jiki umareru n' de, nan da ka ochitsukanai n' da.

I just can't seem to settle down what with the baby due any day now.

n' toko (んとこ) Corruption of *no tokoro* (の所): "Where, one's."

君んとこの会社は不景気で、ここんとこ業績不振に悩んでるな。

Kimi n' toko no kaisha wa fu-keiki de, koko n' toko gyōseki-fushin ni nayande 'ru na.

Sales are down at your place, aren't they, what with the recession and all.

あそこんとこに用紙がありますから、自分で記入してください。

Asoko n' toko ni yōshi ga arimasu kara, jibun de kinyū shite kudasai.

There're some forms right over there, so go ahead and fill one out yourself.

tte (って) Gruff colloquial corruption of *to itte*. Used between two nouns or noun phrases: "Called, known as."

フランスって国、前から一度尋ねてみたいと思っていたとこだ。

Furansu tte kuni, mae kara ichido tazunete mitai to omotte ita toko da.

France, now there's a place I've always wanted to see.

あんたってばかね。あたしが自殺するって本当に信じてたのね。

Anta tte baka ne. Atashi ga jisatsu suru tte hontō ni shinjite 'ta no ne.

You big dummy. How could you really think I'd go and kill myself?

tena (てな) Corruption of *-to iu yō na*. Used mainly by men: "Like, something like, such as."

あなたのためなら死んだっていい、てなこと言われてみたいよ。

Anata no tame nara shinda tte ii, tena koto iwarete mitai yo.

Just once, I wish someone would say something to me like, "I'd die for you."

おれが社長令嬢と結婚する、てなわけにはいくわけがないよな。

Ore ga shachō-reijō to kekkon suru, tena wake ni wa iku wake ga nai yo na.

I guess there's no way I could end up marrying the president's daughter.

-terā (てらあ) A corruption of *-te iru wa*, with the modern meaning of *-te iru nā*. Appears as the end of a sentence following a verb and expressing the speaker's surprise, disdain, or contempt. Also *-derā* according to the previous verb: e.g., *bīru o nonderā*. Characteristic of rough language used predominantly by men.

自称プレーボーイの長嶺君が、すげえブスとつき合ってらあ。ダサイな。

Jishō purēbōi no Nagamine-kun ga, sugē busu to tsukiatterā. Dasai na.

Nagamine calls himself a playboy, but you oughta see the skag he's goin' out with. Dude's such a geek.

わざわざ説明されなくても、カメラの扱い方ぐらい知ってらあ。

Wazawaza setsumei sarenakute mo, kamera no atsukai-kata gurai shitterā.

Whadaya think, I don't even know how to use a camera? You don't have to explain that shit to me.

tsū (つう) A corruption of *to iu*; same as *chū* (see above). Used mainly by young people in the Tokyo area: "Called, named; of."

おまえ、なんつう口のききかたするんだ。もう一度言いなおせ。

Omae, nan tsū kuchi no kiki-kata suru n' da. Mō ichido iinaose.

Just who do you think you are, talking like that? Try it again, with a little respect this time.

企画書は出せばいいっつうもんじゃない。よく考えて持ってこい。

Kikaku-sho wa daseba ii 'tsū mon ja nai. Yoku kangaete motte koi.

The idea's not to just turn in any old proposal. Bring it back after you've given it some thought.

yagaru (やがる) A corruption of *agaru* (上がる) in a similar sense. Following a verb at the end of a sentence, expresses contempt or disdain for the behavior of the listener or a third party. Vulgar male usage.

弟のやつ、宿題もしないで寝やがる。たたき起こしてやるぞ。

Otōto no yatsu, shukudai mo shinai de nete yagaru. Tataki okoshite yaru zo.

Fuckin' little brother went to sleep without doin' his homework. I'm gonna roust that sucker.

あのヤクザ、こっちに来やがった。すぐ逃げないとからまれそうだぞ。

Ano yakuza, kotchi ni kiyagatta. Sugu nigenai to karamaresō da zo.

That yakuza's headed this way. We'd better split, or else we'll be mixin' it up with him.

☞ *Ketsukaru* is the Kansai equivalent, as in *Nani iūte ketsukaru* (何言うてけつかる) "What are you mouthin' off about now, asshole!"

Index

POWER JAPANESE SERIES

An ongoing series of compact, affordable guides dedicated to the learning and improvement of essential language skills.

Other titles in this series:

ALL ABOUT KATAKANA

Anne Matsumoto Stewart

A quick, easy way to learn *katakana* and increase your vocabulary at the same time.

144 pages; paperback

ALL ABOUT PARTICLES

Naoko Chino

Discover new particles and recall the old while learning proper usage.

128 pages; paperback

FLIP, SLITHER, & BANG
Japanese Sound and Action Words

Hiroko Fukuda

Master crucial Japanese language skills quickly and easily through sample dialogs of everyday situations.

128 pages; paperback

"BODY" LANGUAGE

Jeffrey G. Garrison

Have fun learning common idioms and expressions referring to the human body.

128 pages; paperback

GONE FISHIN'

New Angles on Perennial Problems

Jay Rubin

Clears up, with intelligence and wit, the most problematic aspects of the language.

128 pages; paperback

INSTANT VOCABULARY THROUGH PREFIXES AND SUFFIXES

Timothy J. Vance

Learn hundreds of new words by modifying your existing vocabulary.

128 pages; paperback

JAPANESE-LANGUAGE LEARNING MATERIALS

FROM KODANSHA INTERNATIONAL, LTD.

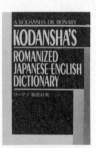

KODANSHA'S ROMANIZED JAPANESE-ENGLISH DICTIONARY

An easy-to-use, comprehensive dictionary for learners with 16,000 entries listed alphabetically, and defined for English speakers.

688 pages; Vinyl flexibinding

KODANSHA'S COMPACT KANJI GUIDE

A compact Japanese-English character dictionary based on the 1,945 Jōyō ("common use") Kanji. 20,000 practical words.

928 pages; Vinyl flexibinding

THE COMPLETE GUIDE TO EVERYDAY KANJI

Yaeko S. Habein and Gerald B. Mathias

A systematic guide to remembering and understanding the 1,945 Jōyō ("common use") *Kanji*.

344 pages; paperback